A bounty OF bead + wire EARRINGS

A bounty OF bead + wire EARRINGS

50 fun, fast JEWELRY projects

NATHALIE MORNU

LARK CRAFTS

An Imprint of Sterling Publishing Co., Inc.
New York

WWW.LARKCRAFTS.COM

Editor
Nathalie Mornu

Art Director
Carol Morse Barnao

Cover Designer
Pamela Norman

Editorial Assistant
Abby Haffelt

Art Interns
Maegan Zigarevich
Jessica Yee

Library of Congress Cataloging-in-Publication Data

Mornu, Nathalie.
  A bounty of bead & wire, earrings : 50 fun, fast jewelry projects / Nathalie Mornu. -- 1st ed.
    p. cm.
  Includes index.
  ISBN 978-1-4547-0018-0 (pbk. : alk. paper)
  1. Beadwork. 2. Earrings. 3. Jewelry making. I. Title.
  TT860.M6676 2011
  739.27--dc22

                              2011001858

10 9 8 7 6 5 4 3 2 1

First Edition

Published by Lark Crafts
An Imprint of Sterling Publishing Co., Inc.
387 Park Avenue South, New York, NY 10016

© 2011, Lark Crafts, an Imprint of Sterling Publishing Co., Inc.

This book is comprised of materials from the following Lark Crafts and Sterling Publishing titles, with all text, photography, and illustrations © Lark Crafts, unless otherwise specified:
Bead & Fiber Jewelry © 2008; *Beading Vintage-Style Jewelry* © 2007; *Beading with Charms* © 2007
Beading with Filigree, text © 2008, Cynthia Deis; *Beading with Gemstones*, text © 2007, Valérie MacCarthy;
Beading with Pearls © 2008; *Beading with World Beads* © 2009; *Bead Love* © 2006
Boutique Bead & Wire Jewelry, text © 2008, Melody MacDuffee; *Contemporary Bead & Wire Jewelry* © 2006
Dazzling Bead & Wire Crafts © 2005, Prolific Impressions and Sterling Publishing
Elegant Wire Jewelry, text © 2007, Kathleen Ann Frey
Metal Jewelry Made Easy © 2009, Prolific Impressions and Sterling Publishing
30-Minute Earrings © 2010; The Weekend Crafter: Beading © 1998

Distributed in Canada by Sterling Publishing,
c/o Canadian Manda Group, 165 Dufferin Street
Toronto, Ontario, Canada M6K 3H6

Distributed in the United Kingdom by GMC Distribution Services,
Castle Place, 166 High Street, Lewes, East Sussex, England BN7 1XU

Distributed in Australia by Capricorn Link (Australia) Pty Ltd.,
P.O. Box 704, Windsor, NSW 2756 Australia

If you have questions or comments about this book, please contact:
Lark Crafts, 67 Broadway, Asheville, NC 28801
828-253-0467

Manufactured in China

All rights reserved

ISBN 13: 978-1-4547-0018-0

For information about custom editions, special sales, and premium and corporate purchases, please contact the Sterling Special Sales Department at 800-805-5489 or specialsales@sterlingpub.com.

For information about desk and examination copies available to college and university professors, submit requests to academic@larkbooks.com. Our complete policy can be found at www.larkcrafts.com.

contents

introduction

Your face is the first thing people notice. It only makes sense to call a little more attention to it by wearing some pretty earrings. Why not have fun by making those earrings yourself? Beads, lovely beads—they sparkle, they shine, they glint, and they twinkle. And they're easy to combine with wire, too.

Whether you're looking to create a sophisticated ear bauble or casual dangles, the 50 projects in *A Bounty of Bead & Wire: Earrings* offer something for everyone. There's the Hoopla earrings on page 66, which feature faceted gemstone beads—in luxe lapis lazuli—strung on simple yet elegant wire hoops. With their Asian-themed beads, the Good Earth earrings (page 65) will appeal to the flower child in you. The Red Lantern earrings (page 32) are three-tiered stunners with ruby glass beads that dangle from filigree bead caps. Prefer a spare look? Go with the Rough Ruby Nuggets (page 53). For something more fancy, check out the Tango chandeliers on page 45.

If you're an experienced beader, you'll appreciate these polished designs. But the real beauty of this book is that even a complete beginner can use it to craft beautiful earrings every time. The basics section offers you detailed descriptions of the star materials—beads and wire—and explains everything you need to know to complete each project, including tools, step-by-step technique photos, and optional alternatives to personalize your earrings. The projects are simple and fast to make, and the instructions guide you every step of the way, so you're guaranteed success.

Whether you're looking to make an accessory to match your favorite outfit or the perfect birthday gift for a friend, this book delivers. And when people admire your earrings, just tell them, "I made them myself!"

basics

For an artist, it's no stretch to conceive of wire as a linear element, and beads as dots or points. The beauty of the projects in this book is that each transforms these simple building blocks into chic earrings to wear as ornaments.

Carved bone, silver Thai beads, semiprecious gem nuggets, glistening crystal, vintage plastic, artists' beads, electroformed silver—the incredible variety available today is an indication of the continued, and still growing, interest in beads. Whether you haunt craft shops, go to bead shows, or travel the Net, beads that were once hard to find are quickly at your fingertips, and better yet, more affordable than ever.

MATERIALS

This section describes the basic items and equipment that are essential for making jewelry. The real fun comes in when shopping for your beads and wire; it's a little like taking a trip around the globe: you'll find African trade beads, lampworked glass crafted in India, cloisonné treasures made in China, shimmering Austrian crystal, and wire from, well, all over.

Beads

If you've never worked in this medium before, you're in for some pleasant hours of bead browsing—the hardest part is stopping! Most beads are organized in stores by their material, shape, and diameter.

Sizing

Beads are measured in millimeters. For those of you more accustomed to inches, the comparison chart should help you as you shop (figure 1). You can buy beads individually or in strands. Most strands are 16 inches (40.6 cm) long, with the number of beads on each strand determined by individual size.

Holes: Orientation and Diameter

Some beads need to be tested for fit on the wire or findings of choice. The position and size of the hole, or drill, in the bead, crystal, or pearl will have a huge effect on the finished piece because it determines how the object will be attached.

A bead with a hole that runs from the top to the bottom is called length-drilled. This is the most common treatment. You can assume that supplies lists are calling for a length-drilled bead, crystal, or stone if nothing is specified. When the hole is through the width, it is a horizontal drill. As the name implies, a top-drilled (or tip-drilled) bead, crystal, or pearl has a hole near the top.

The size of a hole is another concern. Some beads may need larger holes if your project requires stronger, thicker wire. Some suppliers might let you request a strand that includes beads with larger holes. Depending on the product, the hole size may not be consistent from one bead to the next. If necessary, you can drill, or ream, a hole to make it larger.

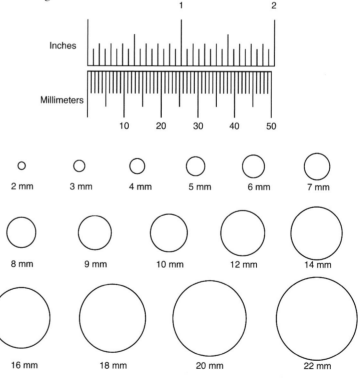

figure 1

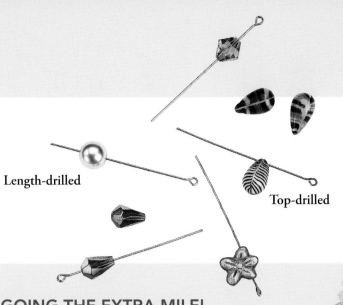

Length-drilled

Top-drilled

GOING THE EXTRA MILE!
Reaming Beads

When the hole in a bead is too small to fit onto a wire, headpin, or finding, you can make it larger. It is not worth the effort to ream a seed bead, or any other inexpensive bead. Semiprecious stones or artisan beads, on the other hand, are ideal candidates for this process.

1. Stick the bead onto a small piece of poster putty.

2. Using a manual or electric bead reamer, begin reaming. Reamer tips are diamond-coated, so using it when dry will, too often, wear off this surface. To avoid this, try to keep the tip wet. If you're using a manual tool, you can work with the reamer while its tip is submerged in a shallow bowl of water or held under running water. Never do this with an electric reamer. Instead, dip the drill bit in a small cup of water whenever it feels like the bit is sticking. Work slowly for maximum control, and do not push too hard. Stop when you're midway through the bead's hole.

3. Remove the putty, flip the bead over and stick the putty on the opposite side. Finish reaming the hole from the newly exposed opening.

    Designer's Tip: Do not ream crystals. They shatter easily. Instead, choose a wire or jump ring to fit the hole.

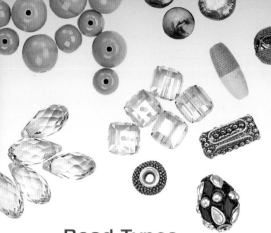

Bead Types and Shapes

The variety of beads on the market today can overwhelm a beginner—and even an intermediate to advanced beader. Familiarizing yourself with the different types and shapes can be very helpful in narrowing down your choices when looking for that perfect bead.

If you can't find beads to replicate the projects in this book, by all means, purchase different styles. Bear in mind that in doing so, you may achieve a completely different look, and you'll need to make certain that your selections match the bead sizes specified in the instructions.

Art glass

Axe head—fan shaped or one-quarter of a circle

Bali-style metal

Baroque pearls

Barrel

Bicone—two cones fused end to end

Branch—organically shaped, cropped frangia

Brick—rectangular-shaped

Briolette—pear-shaped with triangular or diamond shaped facets

Bugle—long cylinder with larger piercing

Button—any shape slightly puffed or domed

Cathedral—stepped ends with a faceted ring around the middle

Charms—made with lively, detailed images, mementos, words, symbols, or decorative designs

Chevron—wide V shape

Chinese cinnabar

Chip—roughly cut chunks

Cloisonné

Coin—flat shape, or actual coin

Cone

Coral

Crow—traditional rounded beads with large holes, similar to pony beads, but bigger

Crystal—if it's labeled AB, that refers to the Aurora Borealis coating, which gives a rainbow-like effect

Cube

Cupolini—polished chips that are shaped, sized, and grouped accordingly

Cushion—puffed square, sometimes nicknamed squoval

Cylinder

Diamond

Die—side-drilled cube, as opposed to corner-drilled

Disk—a slice of a cylinder

Domed—any geometric shape with curvilinear sides

Donut—any shape with an equilateral cutout that mimics the perimeter shape

Dotted lines—round pony beads with ridges formed by lines of dots

Double tube—tube with another shorter tube layered around it

Drop—fattened teardrop

Druk—to the eye, perfectly round glass beads with no seam lines

Drum—can have straight sides or curved sides to resemble an hourglass

Enameled Moroccan

Faceted—any shape where curved lines have been squared off into facets (e.g., faceted rounds, faceted oval, faceted cube)

Faceted round—small round bead with flattened

Fiber-covered

Filigree—a decorative network of surface lines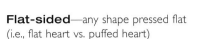

Flat-sided—any shape pressed flat (i.e., flat heart vs. puffed heart)

Flatter cube—traditional cube with flattened edges that make extra facets

Frangia—Italian for fringe, these are groupings of long, branched beads

Freshwater stick

German marble

Go-go—round, off-center donut; also called magatama

Heishi—denotes disks cut from shell

Hex rondelle—rondelle with six faceted sides

Horn

Indian

Lentil—small, flat, and round

Long drop—pierced from tip to tip rather than across the top

Marquise—low, pointed oval, as in a marquise-cut gem

Melon—a fat, round bead with rounded ridges (or cast lines), mimicking melon skin

Mosaic—smaller barrel with rounded ends

Nugget—organically shaped lump

Nut (drilled and polished)

Pear

Pearl

Pebble—a pinched oval

Peruvian

Point—organically shaped, resembling a long crystal

Pony—traditional rounded beads with large holes, similar to crow beads, but smaller

Porcelain

Pressed glass

Puffed—fattened, softened version of original shape (e.g., puffed rectangle, puffed disk, etc.)

Resin

Rice

Rococo—organically shaped; mostly denotes pearls that are flat on one end

Rondelle—flat and circular

Rounded drop—highly faceted narrow drop with points more rounded than sharp

Seven-layer chevron—from eighteenth-century Venice

Sharp drop—drop cut so all facets join at a common, prominent point

Shield—slightly curvilinear triangle

Spindle—resembles a fused set of graduated rondelle beads

Square

Squared tube—squared cylinder with rounded corners and ends

Starflake—a six-pointed snowflake that can interlock with others

Stick—as a group, denotes pearls that are long and flattened, also known as baroque

Stone

Tablet—elongated puffed rectangle with rounded edges

Teardrop

Tribead—three nodules extending from a common pierced center; each bead can interlock with other tribeads

Trumpet—uniformly ridged cone with wide flare at one end

Tube

Twist—any shape twisted a half to a full turn

Vase—a traditional round bead with a ring of glass around each end piercing

Venetian trade

West African lost wax

Wheel—basic wheel shape with diamond-faceted, outward-facing sides

Wire

Traditionally, wire made from sterling silver or gold has been a popular choice for bead and wire jewelry, but many other wire products may be used, too. Metal craft wire is now available in a wide variety of colors; relative newcomers include anodized and dyed metals, such as aluminum or niobium. Still, other kinds of wire include steel, brass, nickel, copper, and even platinum. Unlike these more malleable metals, super-springy memory wire, made from base metal or stainless steel, can be stretched and permanently bent, but it will always retain its initial coiled silhouette.

Whatever the metal, most wire comes in a large range of sizes and shapes or profiles. Gauge is a scale of measurement that indicates a wire's diameter—the higher the numeral, the finer the wire—however, memory wire is sold in sizes to fit the neck, wrist, or finger and is the exception to gauge measurements. The Key to Wire Gauges chart on page 139 lists some helpful information about wire gauges and their specifications, both metric and standard.

Using gauges other than those listed in the instructions is fine, but keep in mind that very thin wire, though easier to shape, isn't strong enough for a lot of heavy beads, and very thick wire isn't suitable for small-scale designs—not to mention the limitation of the size of a bead's hole. Wires of the same gauge will all feel a bit different to manipulate because some metals are softer than others.

Above (from top) are various gauges and types of wire: gold wire, silver wire, and memory wire

Left: square and round wire profiles

However, wire stiffens a bit as you work with it, adding more support to your work. This process is called work-hardening. If wire gets handled too much, it becomes brittle and breaks.

Silver and gold wires are made and sold in different hardnesses: dead soft, soft, and half hard. In many cases, our designers have recommended the appropriate silver or gold wire hardness for their projects; when in doubt, use half-hard wire. Avoid dead-soft wire. It's difficult to work with and won't retain shaping or angles.

Many of the projects in this book use sterling silver wire, but wire made from an alloy—a blend of less expensive metals—is an acceptable substitute, especially for jewelry for everyday wear or for working an unfamiliar design or technique. It's a great idea to use practice wire of a similar gauge and hardness if you plan to make a piece of jewelry from very expensive wire. Any inexpensive alloy wire will do.

Depending on the metal, wire is sold many different ways: on spools, in prepackaged coils, by weight, and by length. Look for various types in jewelry supply shops, craft retailers, and in certain areas of hardware stores, including the electrical supply and framing departments. The Internet is also a vast resource for wire of every kind.

In addition to the plain round variety, wire is made with different cross-section profiles, such as square, half round, and triangular. Some wire companies sell lengths of pre-twisted single-strand wire, or you can make your own. Twisted wire is also created when two lengths of non-round wire are twisted together for a beaded or rippled effect. It's possible to alternate links of round, flat, and twisted wire with stunning results.

Findings

In beading, you'll often need more than just beads and wire to create your final piece. Findings serve as those extra ingredients. They're usually made of metal and are meant to connect, finish, and embellish your jewelry designs.

Bead caps fit over the tops and bottoms of beads. They're used to finish a strand of beads or as spacers between beads.

Chain is made up of connected loops of wire. The loops can come in several forms, including round, oval, twisted, and hammered.

Connectors allow you to make the transition from one beaded strand to many strands.

Crimp tubes and crimp beads secure the ends of beading wire to keep the beads on while providing means for attaching an ear wire or finding.

Eye pins are straight pieces of wire with a simple loop at one end. They're used to make beaded links.

Head pins are used for stringing beads to make dangles. Simple head pins are composed of a straight wire with a tiny disk at one end to hold beads in place. Ball-end head pins have a ball at the end instead of a disk.

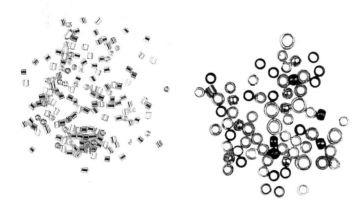

Ear wires are the findings you use to make pierced earrings. They include a jump ring–like loop onto which you can add an earring dangle. They come in different shapes, including French ear wires, which look like upside-down U shapes; hoops, which are simply rings of thin wire with a catch to hold them closed; and lever backs, which are much like French ear wires, but have a safety catch on the back.

Jump rings are circular loops of wire used to connect beadwork to findings or findings to findings. They come in open and soldered-closed versions. You can find them at any beading or craft retail store in a variety of colors and metals, or you can make your own with any wire you have on hand (see Going the Extra Mile! on page 24).

Spacers are small, plain elements used to separate and set off the beads in a design.

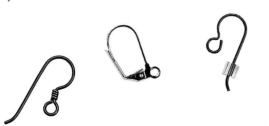

earrings
around the world

China

Laos

Spain

Myanmar

United States

United Kingdom

Italy

Germany

15

Chain-nose pliers

Safety glasses

Flat-nose pliers

TOOLS

Making bead and wire earrings requires surprisingly few tools, and all are pretty low-tech. As with other jewelry-making materials, make sure to buy the best type you can afford.

Pliers have either serrated or smooth surfaces on their jaws. Smooth-jawed pliers are preferable for jewelry making, since they won't scratch the materials you use. If you're going to invest in a set of pliers, make sure they're smooth jawed. If you want to use the serrated pliers you already have, you can wrap the jaws with surgical adhesive tape to protect your work—just be careful to avoid getting any of the adhesive on your materials.

Chain-nose pliers feature jaws that are flat on the inside, but taper to a point on the outside. This type of pliers also comes in a bent version used for grasping hard-to-reach places.

Flat-nose pliers feature jaws that are flat on the inside and have a square nose.

Round-nose pliers feature cylindrical jaws that taper to a very fine point.

Crimping pliers attach crimp beads and crimp tubes to beading wire. See page 27 for instructions on how to use these pliers.

Round-nose pliers

Crimping pliers

Jeweler's wire cutters have very sharp blades that come to a point. One side of the pliers leaves a V-shaped cut; the other side leaves a flat, or flush, cut.

Safety glasses are important to wear when making metal jewelry. They protect your eyes from flying wire pieces.

Dowels and knitting needles are called for in this book to make wire coils and form wire into ear wires.

Emery boards are used in jewelry making for sanding wire smooth.

Jigs are made up of a flat board with movable pegs. The pegs are placed at desired intervals to help bend wire into perfect loops. You can purchase one commercially, or easily make your own. Just a few of the earrings in this book require a jig, so this isn't a required tool.

Mandrels are any straight or tapered rod around which you can wrap wire to shape it into coils. It's an essential tool for making jump rings, the loops in closures, or uniformly sized units, for links. You can buy metal rods or simply use a nail, pen, or any household item with a dowel-like shape.

Metal hand files, or needle files, have very fine teeth. They're used for smoothing wire ends.

Tape measures and rulers are used to determine where to cut wire and thread. They're also helpful for checking jewelry lengths and bead and finding sizes. Choose one that has both standard and metric markings.

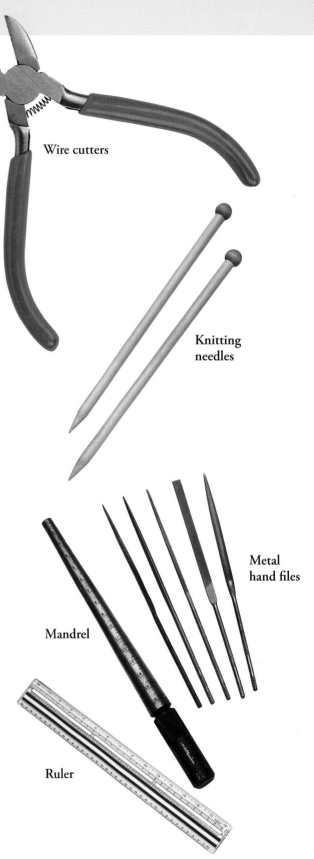

Wire cutters

Knitting needles

Metal hand files

Mandrel

Ruler

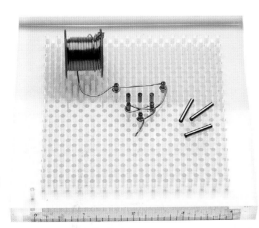

Jig

earrings around the world

Japan

Kenya

Namibia

Turkey

Italy

India

Nepal

South Africa

GOING THE EXTRA MILE!
Handy Extras

You can make all the projects in this book with the tools listed on pages 16 and 17, but if you're feeling super-ambitious, check out these handy extras.

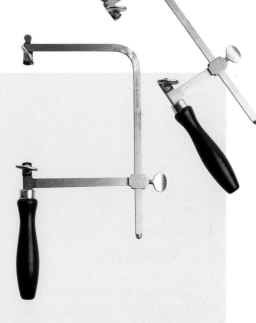

Rubberized round-nose pliers are excellent for making ear wires (page 25). These are not readily available commercially, but you can make them yourself with a pair of standard round-nose pliers and plastic (or rubber) dip from the local hardware store. The dip is a liquid form of plastic that feels like rubber after it dries. Use the dip to coat the jaws, being careful not to coat the hinges. You may need to dip the jaw tips several times to get them thickly coated. Hang the pliers immediately to make sure the coating dries evenly.

Nylon-jaw pliers are the tool to use for flattening wire projects. The rubberized round-nose pliers also work for this, but the jaws of the nylon-jaw pliers are flat and hard, getting the job done more efficiently without damaging your work.

Slide calipers are useful for determining the sizes of stones, beads, and chains. Place the stone or component you want to size between the two jaws of the caliper and slide them tight. The size will be indicated on top of the caliper. This little tool comes in handy when bead shopping for your projects.

A **jeweler's saw** frame is an optional tool for the person who wants to make jump rings. (Little bags of jump rings sell for next to nothing, so there's really nothing wrong with being lazy and purchasing them. Just think of it as a time-saving initiative.) Saw frames have wooden handles and metal jaws, and come in two basic sizes, one with a 60-mm throat and the other with a 100-mm throat. Either size is good. **Jeweler's saw blades** go in the saw frame and come in a range of sizes, made by a number of different manufacturers. Size 3 is the largest and sizes 1/0, 2/0, and 3/0 are smaller. A good basic size for a beginner is 3/0, which can be used for just about any jewelry application. Invest in a good-quality blade; cheap blades break more easily and aren't worth the money saved.

An **eggbeater drill** is useful if it's important to you to make your own jump rings. This tool will enable you to rapidly coil long quantities of wire around a small mandrel.

TECHNIQUES

You'll need a variety of skills to make all the projects in this book, but have no fear. They're relatively simple, and by studying the techniques below, you'll be working like a pro in no time.

Wireworking

Now for the fun: learning how to wrangle wire into a great jewelry design using basic wire techniques. Unless you're already familiar with them, you'll probably want to practice these techniques with a low-cost wire first—it's not easy to straighten wire once it's bent the wrong way.

QUICK TIP: WIRE CONTROL

To keep spooled wire under control, put it in a small plastic storage bag. Pull out a length of wire as needed. If you're working with a coil of wire rather than a spool, wrap a piece of masking tape around it so it can't spring open in all directions. Good-looking jewelry pieces are those with smooth and confident swoops, angles, and curves, made from kink-free wire.

Straightening

To keep it in good condition, wire is stored and sold in coils. Coiling wire saves space, but it's best to straighten out its curve before you begin working with it. To straighten a short length of wire, hold one end of it with chain-nose pliers. Just above the pliers, grasp the wire with a cloth or paper towel to keep your hands clean and to prevent friction burn. Squeezing your fingers slightly, pull the length of wire through them.

If the wire bends or crimps at any time, gently run your finger along it to smooth the kink, or rub the wire over the edge of a table padded with newspaper. Don't smooth a crimp too vigorously, or the wire could break. The more you shape the wire, the more it work-hardens and becomes brittle.

Stringing

Stringing beads is a simple act—simply pass wire through a bead, and you've got it! It's how you arrange beads on the stringing material that creates masterpieces—that's what takes practice.

Coiling

Coiling, or tightly wrapping, wire is primarily used in this book for attaching one wire to another, creating decorative coils, and making jump rings. Start by grasping the base—a thick wire, dowel, or knitting needle—tightly in one hand. Hold the wrapping wire with your other hand and make one wrap. Reposition your hands so you can continue to wrap the wire around the base wire, making tight revolutions (photo 1).

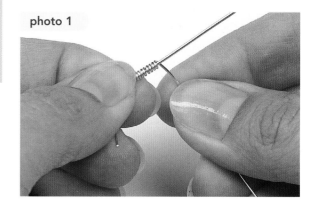

photo 1

Spiraling

Spiraling is great technique to add depth and embellishment to your design, or even create the focal point of your piece.

1. Use the tip of a pair of round-nose pliers to curve one end of the wire into a half-circle or hook shape about ⅛ inch (3 mm) in diameter (see figure 2).

figure 2

2. Use the very tips of the pliers to curve the end of the wire tightly into itself, as shown in figure 3, aiming to keep the shape round rather than oval. Hold the spiral in flat- or chain-nose pliers and push the loose end of the wire against the already-coiled form (see figure 4); as you continue, reposition the wire in the pliers as needed.

figure 3   figure 4

Making Simple Loops

1. Use chain-nose pliers to make a 90° bend ⅜ inch (1 cm) from the end of the wire; or, if you're using the loop to secure a bead (as with a bead dangle), make the 90° bend right at the top of the bead and cut the wire ⅜ inch (1 cm) from the top of the bead (photo 2).

2. Use round-nose pliers to grasp the wire end and roll the pliers until the wire touches the 90° bend (photo 3).

Making Wrapped Loops

1. Use chain-nose pliers to make a 90° bend in the wire 2 inches (5.1 cm) from one wire end or ¼ inch (6 mm) from the top of a bead (photo 4).

2. Using round-nose pliers to grasp the bend, shape the wire over the top jaw (photo 5), and swing it underneath to form a partial loop (photo 6).

photo 2

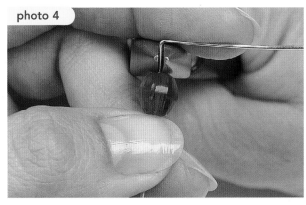

photo 3

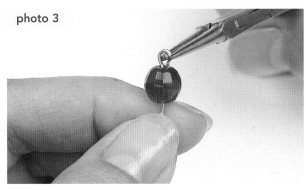

photo 4

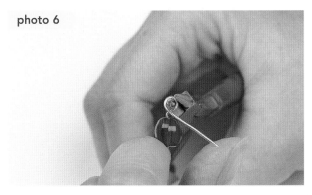

photo 6

photo 5

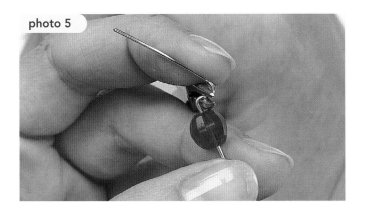

photo 7

3. Use chain-nose pliers or your fingers to wrap the wire in a tight coil down the stem (photo 7). Then trim the excess wire close to the wrap and use chain-nose pliers to tighten the wire end.

QUICK TIP: LOOPS

Throughout the book, you'lll notice that the project instructions sometimes say to bend the wire 45°, rather than 90°. This bend keeps the loop centered above the bead and prevents it from veering to one side just as well as the 90° bend (photo 8).

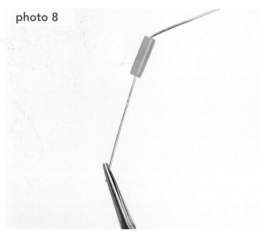

photo 8

Making Triangular Wraps

This wrap looks great on a bead that's drilled through the width or tip-drilled, or a bicone you want to position horizontally.

1. Cut a piece of wire 2 inches (5 cm) long. With the flat-nose pliers, bend the last ½ inch (1.3 cm) of the wire upwards. Thread a bead onto the wire.

2. Fold up the other side of the wire until the pieces cross directly above the bead (figure 5).

3. Take the chain-nose pliers to the base of the longer wire, and bend it back down a bit. Use the round-nose pliers to make a simple loop (figure 6).

4. Finish the piece by wrapping the end of the longer wire around the base several times. Snip off the excess wire and file the end. You can also tuck the end underneath the last loop.

When attaching with this type of wrap, make sure the direction of the loop brings attention to the bead instead of the wire. If you've already completed your loop and it's not facing the direction you prefer, simply grip the loop with round-nose pliers and give it a small, additional twist to make the loop either forward-facing or side-facing, whichever's needed for your piece. Following up with this small yet important detail will allow the bead to be the focus of your design.

figure 5

figure 6

Forward-facing link

Side-facing link

earrings around the world

France

Holland

Nepal

Georgia

Mexico

Greece

Myanmar

Russia

Opening and Closing Jump Rings

Always open a jump ring with two pairs of pliers, one positioned on each side of the split. Push one pair of pliers away from you, and pull the other one toward you (photo 9). This way the ring will open laterally instead of horizontally, which can weaken the wire. You should open any other wire loop you work with the same way.

Working with Purchased Earring Findings

There are various types of prefabricated ear wire findings you can use to make the projects in this book. Attaching items to these findings is very simple.

1. Grasp the loop on the finding with chain-nose pliers, and twist very slightly to one side. Never pull the loop open; instead, gently twist it to one side.

2. Place the chain or a stone on the open loop and close it, again using the chain-nose pliers.

You can see how easy it is to substitute the findings as you wish when you make your own pieces of jewelry.

photo 9

GOING THE EXTRA MILE!
Making Your Own Jump Rings

To make your own jump rings, simply wind a length of wire tightly around a mandrel. If you want to make a lot of jump rings at once, you might consider using an eggbeater drill to quickly do the job.

1. Secure both the mandrel and one end of the wire tightly in the tool's jaws. As you turn the handle, hold the wire close to the mandrel. Whether you use a drill or not, keep the rounds of wire as straight and as close to each other as possible.

2. After you've wound all the wire, slide the coil you've just formed off the mandrel and trim the ends. Use wire cutters, in exactly the same position each time, to free a fully circular ring— no more, no less—from the coil. *One last tip:* It's tempting to use your fingers to pry open a jump ring, but avoid splitting your nails by using two pairs of flat-nose pliers instead.

GOING THE EXTRA MILE!
Making Your Own Ear Wires

1. To make an ear wire, use wire cutters to cut a 2½-inch (6.4 cm) length of 22-gauge wire. Use round-nose pliers to grip the wire ¾ inch (1.9 cm) from the end. Wrap the wire around the pliers to form a circle (photo 10). Grip the loop with the chain-nose pliers and twist the two wire ends around each other. Cut the excess from the shorter wire (photo 11).

2. Using rubberized round-nose pliers, wrap the wire, starting at the twisted end, around one jaw of the pliers to create the rounded shape of an earring loop (photo 12).

3. Add a little flip at the end of the wire as a finishing detail. To create this effect, use large pliers to grip the tip of the wire and bend it up very slightly (photo 13).

4. Use wire cutters to cut the wire to the desired length.

In most cases, the components added to ear wires, such as stones or bead links, are attached permanently by slipping them on in step 1 after you've made the first wire. Doing this keeps the component permanently attached to the ear wire, but it also means the design can't be changed unless you cut through the twisted loop.

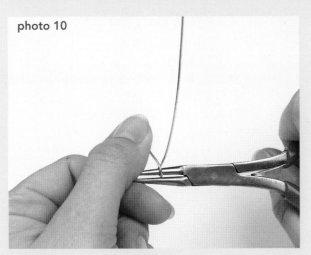
photo 10

photo 12

photo 11

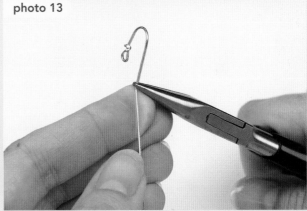
photo 13

earrings

around the world

Canada

Middle East

Spain

Brazil

United States

Kenya

Vietnam

South Africa

Using a Jig

Jigs are especially handy because they allow you to quickly create multiple wire designs, all of them identical. A jig is basically a flat surface with equidistant holes. You place pegs in these holes to form the desired pattern, and then you wrap wire around them to form a looped wire design (photo 14). Be sure to experiment with inexpensive wire until you're pleased with the results of your jig work, then switch to precious-metal wire to make your jewelry design.

Finishing Off Your Wires

When you're done with a piece of wire, clip the tails and press them down so there will be no sharp ends sticking out of your finished piece that could scratch or stab you or get caught in your clothes.

1. First, clip the tails of your wire off at the front side of your piece with wire cutters that are fairly small, sharp, and come to a fine point. Sometimes you'll be forced by the density of wires and/or motifs in the area where you're clipping to go in with the point of your cutters. Otherwise, always clip your wires by placing the back side of your cutters right up against the stem, branch, motif, or frame the wires are wrapped around.

2. Next, press the clipped tails down with your flat-nose pliers, rotating them gently in the same direction that the wires were being twisted or wrapped. Then run your fingers across the area to check for sharp ends. If you find some, keep pressing them down or clip them a bit more.

Crimping

Crimping is a technique used to attach wire to a finding.

1. String one crimp bead and then the finding. Pass the wire end back through the crimp bead in the opposite direction.

2. Next, slide the crimp bead against the finding so it's snug, but not so tight that the wire can't move freely. Squeeze the crimp bead in the U-shaped notch—the notch furthest from the tip— of a pair of crimping pliers (photo 15).

3. Turn the crimp bead at a 90° angle, and nestle it into the notch closest to the tip of the crimping pliers. Gently squeeze the bead so it collapses on itself, into a nicely-shaped tube (photo 16).

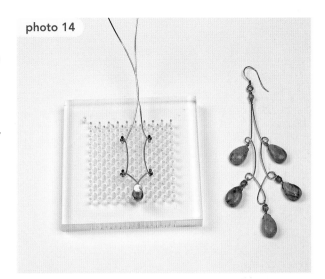

photo 14

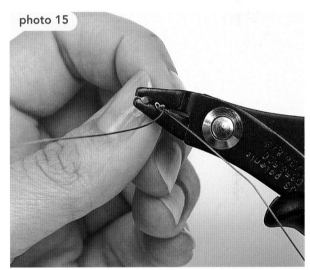

photo 15

photo 16

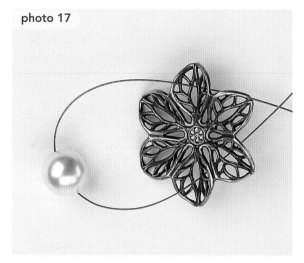

photo 17

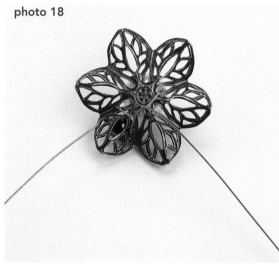

photo 18

photo 19

Sewing Beads to Filigree

Flexible beading wire is the best option when attaching beads to filigree—the wire knots easily and won't damage your fingers. Always try to match the color of the wire to the filigree. This will ensure that any exposed sewing wire blends in and isn't noticed, much like matching your thread when sewing on a button! This technique can create a mess on the back of the filigree, with the knots and tail strands everywhere, so you may want to add another piece of filigree to the back side of your design.

1. Cut the required amount of beading wire and string on one bead, leaving a 4-inch (10.2-cm) tail. Working from the front of the filigree, push both ends of the wire through the filigree holes where specified in the instructions (photo 17).

2. Tie a secure square knot on the back of the filigree (photo 18). A square knot (figure 7) is made by forming an overhand knot with both ends of the stringing material, right end over left end. Repeat this, passing the left end over the right end to make the knot tight and secure.

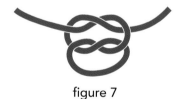

figure 7

3. Pass the long end of the wire up through the filigree to exit where specified in the instructions (photo 19). Slip on a bead and pass the wire down through the filigree to the back of the filigree.

4. Repeat this sewing action until the filigree is beaded as required (photo 20). Tie the wire ends together in a tight square knot and trim. If you're worried about your knots holding, you can add a drop of glue, but it's usually unnecessary.

photo 20

Working with Chain

Chain is one of the simplest materials to use in jewelry making. The toughest part will be deciding which type to use! After that, all you'll need to do is cut the chain and create your piece.

The lengths of chain you'll need for the projects in this book are specified in each set of directions. Rulers are helpful, but be careful not to rely on them for determining the length of the chain. Instead, always make it a practice to count the links. Counting links is of utmost importance when working with short, paired lengths of chain, such as for earrings. The difference of even one small chain link will make your earring noticeably lopsided. Use a ruler to measure only the first length of chain, then count the links in that segment, and count all additional chain segments to make absolutely certain that each one has exactly the same number of links. After you determine the right length for the piece you are making, pull out your trusty wire cutters and snip.

To attach a chain to wire or a finding, slide one link of the chain (often an end link) onto a wire loop or finding. Generally, the connection is secured with wrapped wire.

Polishing

You can polish your jewelry with a jewelry buffing cloth—sometimes called a rouge cloth—or papers, which are available from most jewelry suppliers. Before using any cleaning solution, test it on a scrap piece of wire first. A tumbler is an option for some pieces *if* they're made of nothing but metal, but make sure you're familiar with its operation and keep in mind that fragile beads aren't suitable for the process.

Taking Time to Plan

One of the hardest steps in beading is making yourself take the time to develop a plan. Who can blame you? When faced with an array of beautiful beads, all you want to do is get to work! But if you like to march to the beat of your own drum, this is an important step. Just think of planning as more fun time you can spend with your beads. Use a bead board or lay them out on a towel so they won't roll around. Place different types and colors of spacer beads between the larger beads. Experiment with some common designs, and arrange and rearrange to your heart's content until you have a design you can't live without.

Although a repeating pattern may sound boring, it's anything but. It's one of the best ways to combine colors and textures with ease. The eye quickly picks up on the pattern and is reassured by it. An asymmetrical design is a wonderful way to give a bit of extra emphasis to a focal bead since the eye will hunt for it when it's placed off center.

Try a symmetrical design when working with unusual beads. This more formal arrangement will be juxtaposed with their quirky qualities to highlight them even more. Random design allows you the most freedom. You can mix and layer textures, or stick to one. You can vary the size of the beads or keep them perfectly in proportion to one another.

As you design, keep in mind who will be wearing the earrings. What's her style? How long should the earrings be? What colors and styles of clothing does she wear, and how will those play off the design?

Choosing Color

When it comes to choosing color, search your memory for tips you might remember from Art 101. Find a color wheel and take it for a spin. Monochromatic? Definitely dramatic. Complementary colors? Opposites attract. Cool? And contained. Warm? Sunny disposition. Mix it up by using secondary colors. Meet the analogous neighbors, or keep it all in the family. Allow yourself to experiment with color combinations that are out of your comfort zone. Try making your favorite outfit be your inspiration—even if it's black and white.

the projects

And now, 50 projects to grace your lobes, bob from your ears, skim your jawline, dangle along your pretty neck, and generally bring attention to your gorgeous face.

red lantern

These earrings want to boogie, but even if you're stuck behind a desk all day, the dagger drops will dance for you—cha-cha-cha—every time you move your head. Attaching the drops with jump rings lets them float freely.

Designer: Cynthia Deis

Finished size: 1½ inches (3.8 cm)

Materials

6 patinaed or raw brass filigree five-point bead caps, 6 mm

30 red glass dagger beads, 3 x 10 mm

10 red glass fire-polished beads, 4 mm

30 patinaed or raw brass jump rings, 4 mm

2 patinaed or raw brass head pins, 1 inch (2.5 cm)

1 pair of patinaed brass ear wires

Patinaed or raw brass 20-gauge wire, 6 inches (15.2 cm)

Clear acrylic spray paint or wax (optional)

Tools

Chain-nose pliers

Round-nose pliers

Wire cutters

Cookie sheet (optional)

Heat gun and heat-proof surface (optional)

Instructions

1. If you can only find raw brass findings, patina them with a heat gun. Lay the wire, head pins, and jump rings on a cookie sheet and separate evenly. Set the cookie sheet on a heat-proof surface. Use a heat gun to apply heat to the findings until they darken. Keep an eye on the color and move the gun around to create an even finish. When all the findings are the preferred color, allow to cool. Seal the pieces with a clear finish coat, wax, or allow the pieces to continue to patina naturally.

2. Open a jump ring and slide on a glass dagger. Connect the ring to one of the openings at the edge of a bead cap (figure 1). Repeat around the bead cap to add five daggers in all. Set aside.

fig. 1

3. Repeat step 2 to make two more embellished caps.

4. Cut a 1½-inch (3.8 cm) length of wire. Form a simple loop at one end of the wire. Slide on one 4-mm bead and one embellished cap from outside to inside. Slip on one 4-mm bead so it nestles inside the embellished cap (figure 2). Form a simple loop to secure the cap and bead. Set aside.

fig. 2

5. Cut a 1½-inch (3.8 cm) length of wire. Form a simple loop at one end of the wire. Slide on one 4-mm bead and one embellished cap from inside to outside. Form a simple loop to secure the cap and bead.

6. Connect the cap links so the longer link attaches to the loop inside the shorter link (figure 3).

fig. 3

7. Slip one 4-mm bead onto a head pin. Slide on the remaining embellished cap from inside to outside. Add a 4-mm bead and form a simple loop to create a dangle.

8. Attach the dangle to the open loop of the longer cap link. Attach an ear wire to the remaining open cap link loop.

9. Repeat all steps to make a second earring.

kokopelli

Use a jig to make delicate loops in sterling silver wire for a swaying pair of turquoise earrings.

Designer: Valérie MacCarthy

Finished size: 4⅜ inches (12.3 cm)

Materials

2 turquoise briolettes, 10 mm

8 turquoise briolettes, 8 mm

8 labradorite beads, 3 mm

15-inch (38.1 cm) length of 22-gauge sterling silver wire

18-inch (45.7 cm) length of 26-gauge sterling silver wire

Tools

Jig

Chain-nose pliers

Round-nose pliers

Wire cutters

Large rubberized round-nose pliers or nylon-jaw pliers

Ruler

Instructions

1. Cut the 22-gauge wire into two segments that are 2½ inches (6.4 cm) long, and two that are 5 inches (12.7 cm) long.

2. Place the pegs on the jig as shown in figure 1.

3. Select one 5-inch (12.7 cm) wire segment and wrap it around the pegs, following the pattern shown in figure 2; leaving an end on the wire about 2½ inches (6.4 cm) long, place the wire against the first peg on the jig. Wrap the wire around the peg, and then follow the pattern around, ending when the wire crosses the other end at the top of the pattern.

4. Carefully remove the wire shape from the jig.

5. Using the chain-nose pliers, grip both wires about 1¼ inches (3.2 cm) above the top loops.

fig. 1

fig. 2

Finish   Start

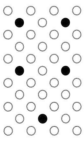

6. Bend the shorter wire 90° to cross the other wire (figure 3).

7. Keeping the chain-nose pliers in place, wrap the bent wire around the straight wire two times. Cut off the excess from this wrapped wire.

8. Place one 3-mm bead on the straight wire and bend the wire above the bead 45°. Make a loop in this wire using the round-nose pliers.

9. Hold this loop with the chain-nose pliers and wrap the wire around to secure.

10. Smooth out the wrapped-wire shape using the rubberized round-nose pliers, or the nylon-jaw pliers, to clamp and flatten the loops between the pliers' jaws. Repeat this process until you've flattened all of the wire shape.

11. Slide the 26-gauge wire through one 10-mm briolette, letting ¾ inch (1.9 cm) extend out the other end. Bend up both wires until they cross tightly. Twist them around each other one full turn. Cut off the shorter wire end.

fig. 3

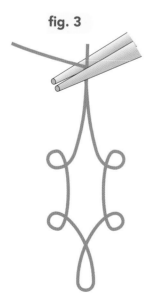

12. Keep the remaining wire extending straight up from the briolette and slide one 3-mm bead onto it. Bend back the wire and wrap it around the round-nose pliers to form a loop.

13. Slide this loop onto the bottom loop in the wrapped-wire shape. Using the chain-nose pliers, hold this loop and wrap the wire around to secure. Cut off the excess wire.

14. Repeat steps 11 through 13 for the bottom two loops of the wrapped-wire shape, and then again for the two top ones, with the difference of deleting the 3-mm beads for the two top loops. Use the 8-mm briolettes for all four of these.

15. To make an earring loop, select one of the 2½-inch (6.4 cm) segments of the 22-gauge wire. Use the round-nose pliers to grip the wire ¾ inch (1.9 cm) from the end. Wrap the wire around the pliers to form a loop. Slide this loop through the top loop of the wire shape.

16. Grip the loop with the chain-nose pliers and twist the two wire ends around each other. Cut off the shorter wire end.

17. Using the rubberized round-nose pliers, hold the wire just above the twist and wrap the wire around one jaw of the pliers to create the rounded shape of an ear wire. Cut the wire to the length you desire. Use these same pliers, or the nylon-jaw pliers, to squeeze the whole earring shape to flatten and straighten it.

18. If you like, add a little flip at the end of the wire as a finishing detail. To create this effect, use the round-nose pliers to grip the tip of the wire and bend it up very slightly.

19. Repeat steps 3 through 18 to make a second earring.

filigree

Designer: Melody MacDuffee

Finished size: 1½ inches (4.4 cm) long and 1¼ inches (3.2 cm) wide, not including ear wires

Materials

12 feet (3.7 m) of 28-gauge gold-filled craft wire or dead-soft wire

32 pink 2- to 3-mm faceted tourmaline rondelle beads

28 round 2-mm garnet beads

24 round 2-mm iolite beads

13 inches (33 cm) of 20-gauge gold-filled half-hard wire

1 pair of gold-filled ear wires

6 gold-filled 4-mm jump rings

Tools

Wire cutters

Round-nose pliers

Chain-nose pliers

Metal file

Romantic hues of garnet, tourmaline, and amethyst sparkle in the gold wires of these elegant earrings.

Instructions

1. Cut a 1-foot (30.5 cm) piece of 28-gauge wire. Using tourmaline for the petals and a garnet for the center, make an Eight-Petal Flower Motif (see box at right). Twist a ¼-inch (6 mm) section of main stem.

2. Using iolite, make a One-Bead Single-Leaf Motif on a ⅜-inch (9.5 mm) branch (see box below). Twist a ¼-inch (6 mm) section of main stem.

3. Repeat step 2 on the same side of the main stem.

4. Using garnets, make a Three-Bead Single-Leaf Motif (see box on next page) on a ⅜-inch (9.5 mm) branch on the same side of the main stem.

5. Using iolite, make a One-Bead Single-Leaf Motif on a ⅜-inch (9.5 mm) branch on the opposite side of the main stem. Twist a ¼-inch (6 mm) section of main stem.

6. Repeat step 5.

7. Repeat step 4 on the opposite side of your main stem.

8. Repeat step 5 twice. Twist an additional 1-inch (2.5 cm) section of main stem.

ONE-BEAD SINGLE-LEAF MOTIF

1. Holding the bead ⅜ inch (9.5 mm) from the main stem, fold the wire back over the bead and, holding the two wires between the thumb and forefinger of your left hand, right up against the base of your bead, give the loop two or three half-twists, just enough to secure it in place.

2. Back your left hand away from the twisted portion bit by bit, still holding the two wires just slightly apart between the thumb and forefinger of your left hand as you twist the motif with your right hand. Continue until the branch is twisted all the way back to the main stem.

EIGHT-PETAL FLOWER MOTIF

1. Add eight tourmaline beads (these are the "petals") to the wire and slide them down to its center point. (**Note:** From this point on, the wires on either side of your beads will be referred to as two separate wires.) Form the beads into a loop, with the wires crossed at its base. Secure the loop in place by wrapping one of the wires (this will be the working wire) around the other (now the dormant wire) twice, very tightly, right up against the base of the loop.

2. Bring the working wire all the way under the loop and then back over, across the front of it. Add a garnet bead and position it in the center of the loop.

3. Holding the two wires between the thumb and forefinger of your left hand, right up against the base of the loop, give the loop two or three half-twists, just enough to secure it in place.

4. Back your left hand away from this twisted portion bit by bit, still holding the two wires just slightly apart between the thumb and forefinger of your left hand as you twist the motif with your right hand, thus beginning the main stem. Keep twisting until the main stem is ¼ inch (6 mm) long.

The finished motif in an alternate colorway.

9. Attach a 10-inch (25.4 cm) piece of 28-gauge wire to the first tourmaline flower you made, by doing the following: Fold this new wire in half, and place the fold across the twisted section at the base of the motif (photo 1 shows this process being done with pale green beads). Bring the wires up behind the motif and thread them, one at a time, down through the motif from front to back, placing them one bead apart from each other. Pull them tight (photo 2). Again, bring the wires up behind the motif and thread them one at a time down through the motif from front to back, placing them one bead apart from each other. You should be able to hold the piece by the new wires without it flopping down as if it were hinged. If it flops, thread the wires through the motif again, changing the locations of the wires a bit to make the "join" more stable. Finally, flip the piece over and twist a ¼-inch (6 mm) section of main stem.

10. Repeat steps 2 through 8 for the other side of the filigree, making it as close to a mirror image of the first side as possible.

11. Repeat steps 1 through 10 to start the other earring.

photo 1

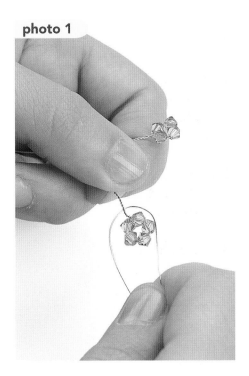

THREE-BEAD SINGLE-LEAF MOTIF

1. Thread three garnets on the wire and slide them toward the main stem. Holding them ⅜ inch (9.5 mm) from the main stem, form them into a loop, with the wires crossed at the loop's base.

The finished motif in an alternate colorway.

2. Secure the loop in place by wrapping the loose end of the working wire twice around the section between this motif and the main stem, wrapping it very tightly and right up against the base of the loop.

3. Back your left hand away from the twisted portion bit by bit, still holding the two wires just slightly apart between the thumb and forefinger of your left hand as you twist the motif with your right hand. Continue until the branch is twisted all the way back to the main stem.

photo 2

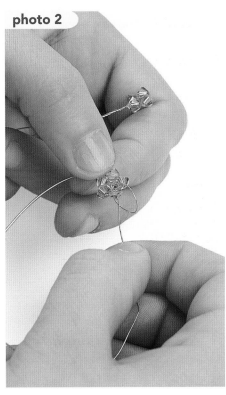

fig. 1

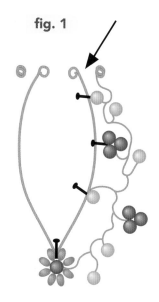

fig. 2

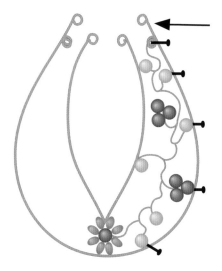

Designer's Tip

If the frame is larger than needed, clip a small portion at a time off of the closed loops, and re-curl them until the frames are the optimal size for the filigree.

12. Refer to figure 1 as you work steps 12 through 15. Cut two 2½-inch (6.4 cm) pieces of the 20-gauge wire. Bend and shape each wire at its center point toward the inside of the wire's natural curve, making a marquise shape that is slightly open at the top. Using round-nose pliers, curl a closed loop toward the back side of the frame at each end of each wire. This completes the inner frames.

13. Using round-nose pliers, tweak the filigrees by gently curving the branches of the motifs as shown in the photograph, shaping them as needed so that they fit around the shape of the inner frames, with the tourmaline flowers centered just under the bottom point of the frames. Curl a loop in the last 1-inch (2.5 cm) twisted section of each filigree, as close in as necessary, keeping the tail end toward the back side of the filigree. Clip the tails.

14. Using short scraps of 28-gauge wire, temporarily "tack" one of the filigrees in place on a frame at each projected point of contact. The points of contact may differ slightly from those in the diagram, as long as the filigree lies comfortably and attractively around the frame.

15. Cut a 2-foot (61 cm) piece of 28-gauge wire, and attach it to the top of one frame just below the closed loop (where the arrow points in the figure) by coiling it around the frame two or three times. This is now the working wire. Coil tightly around the frame until you reach the first point of contact.

16. Remove the first "tacking" wire, and coil the working wire once into the first motif or around the first branch, whichever applies.

17. Continue coiling until you reach the next point of contact.

18. Repeat steps 16 and 17 until all points of contact have been anchored to the frame. Then continue coiling up to the frame's closed loop. Do not clip tails.

19. Repeat steps 13 through 18 for the other earring.

20. Cut the remaining 20-gauge wire in half (two 4-inch [10.2 cm] pieces). Gently form them into "U" shapes that are partially closed at their tops. Curl closed loops at each end of each wire as above. This completes the outer frames.

21. Using round-nose pliers, further tweak the filigrees if necessary so that they fit within the outer frames.

22. Repeat step 14 if desired (see figure 2), though, once you have the hang of coiling, you will find that you save time by skipping this step. By not tacking, you leave a space around the filigree so that you can swing the wire between the frame's closed loops and around the filigree as you coil, instead of having to thread the wire through the filigree every time. Just be sure to check often to see whether you are approaching a desired point of contact.

23. Beginning with a 3-foot (.91 m) length of 28-gauge wire, repeat steps 15 through 19 (see figure 2 again). Check for a good fit between the two frames, clipping portions off the closed loops and recurling them if needed to make the outer hoop a bit smaller. Clip all tails.

24. Using tourmaline for the petals and a garnet for the center, make an Eight-Petal Flower Motif, but this time, make a ⅛-inch (3 mm) length of stem.

25. Using round-nose pliers, wire-wrap a loop at the end of the stem, coiling the wire back down as close as possible to the motif.

26. Bring the wires behind the motif, going past two rondelles (see figure 3). Bring the wires around and through, between the second and third petals, and pull them tight. Twist a ⅛-inch (3 mm) length of stem.

27. Repeat steps 25 and 26 twice, omitting the ⅛-inch (3 mm) length of stem following the final repeat. This completes the flowered top. Curve the first and third wire-wrapped loops downward somewhat.

28. Cut off any extra wire and finish the ends. Attach an ear wire to the second wire-wrapped loop made, making sure that the flower faces forward.

29. Repeat steps 22 through 28 for the other earring.

30. Insert a jump ring through the two loops of one inner frame, and close it securely.

31. Insert a jump ring through this center jump ring, through one of the loops on the outer frame, and through one of the side loops on the flowered top, making sure that the flower is facing forward (see figure 4). Repeat for the other side of the earring.

32. Repeat step 31 for the other earring.

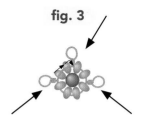

fig. 3

fig. 4

Designer's Tip

As you pull the tops of the frames closed, it may cause the filigrees to bow outward somewhat. If you prefer them flatter, simply tweak the main stems of the filigrees, creating curves that cause the filigrees to pull in a bit.

harmony

Classy smoky quartz nuggets combine with artistically draped chains to make this lovely pair of earrings.

Designer: Valérie MacCarthy

Finished size: 4⅛ inches (10.5 cm)

Materials

2 smoky quartz nuggets, 20 mm

2 smoky quartz briolettes, 5 mm

36-inch (91.4 cm) length of 1.5-mm gold or gold-filled chain

8-inch (20.3 cm) length of 22-gauge gold-filled wire

4-inch (10.2 cm) length of 26-gauge gold-filled wire

Tools

Chain-nose pliers

Round-nose pliers

Wire cutters

Large rubberized round-nose pliers

Ruler

Designer's Tip

This bears repeating: When you're matching lengths of chain, count the links to make sure that each pair or set has exactly the same number of links. This way you'll be certain that they are identical and that both earrings match. A difference of even one tiny link can affect the final appearance of your piece of jewelry.

Instructions

1. Cut the 36-inch (91.4 cm) length of chain into segments. Cut two pieces in each of the following lengths: 2 inches (5.1 cm), 2½ inches (6.4 cm), 3½ inches (8.9 cm), 4½ inches (11.4 cm), and 5½ inches (14 cm). Keep all five sets paired up so you can easily identify the various lengths. *Note:* Before cutting the 2-inch (5.1 cm) chain segments, count the links to make sure you have an odd number. You'll be hanging the earring from the middle link of this chain, which means you need to have an even number of links on either side.

2. Make a basic loop link using the 22-gauge wire and round-nose pliers. Wrap the very end of the wire around the jaw of the round-nose pliers. After making a nearly full loop (figure 1), rotate the pliers so the outside jaw touches the long end of the wire. Clamp down and bend the wire about 45° to center the loop (figure 2). Be sure to keep the loop open a bit, because you'll need to slide on the chain.

fig. 1

fig. 2

3. Select a 20-mm nugget and slide it onto this wire. Bend the wire and repeat the loop from step 2 to match the other side. Clamp the round-nose pliers on the wire as close to the stone as you can get. Wrap the wire around the pliers until you've made a circle. Nudge in the wire cutters to cut off the excess wire, being careful not to cut too much. You now have the foundation, or focal bead, for making the earring.

4. Keeping the spaces in the wire loops facing up (figure 3), place one set of chain segments onto one loop, starting with the 2½-inch (6.4 cm), followed by the 3½-inch (8.9 cm), the 4½-inch (11.4 cm), the 5½-inch (14 cm), and finally the 2-inch (5.1 cm) chain. To place a chain, hold the last link on the chain with the chain-nose pliers and slip it onto one wire loop. Making sure the chain doesn't twist, grab hold of the opposite end of the chain segment you're working with and slide it onto the second loop (figure 4).

5. Repeat step 4 with the remaining four chains.

6. After all the chains are in place, use the round-nose pliers to close the two wire loops. Set aside this part of the earring.

7. Make a wire loop link for one briolette. Using the 24-gauge wire, slide it through the briolette with ¾ inch (1.9 cm) extending out the other side. Bend the wire up on both sides of the stone. Cross the wires so they fit snugly around the top of the stone and, using either your fingers or the chain-nose pliers, twist the wires around. Cut off the shorter wire end.

8. Bend the longer wire 45° just above the twist. Using the round-nose pliers, make a loop. Hold the loop

with the chain-nose pliers and wrap the wire back around the twist. Cut off the excess wire (figure 5). Set aside this part of the earring.

9. Finally, make the earring loop and bring it all together. Using the 22-gauge wire and the round-nose pliers, wrap the wire to create a loop with a short end about ½ inch (1.3 cm) long.

10. First, slide onto this loop the briolette, followed by the middle link in the 2-inch (5.1 cm) chain. Slide the two end links of this chain to the top of the wire loops beside the focal bead.

11. After everything is in place, hold the loop with the chain-nose pliers and twist the wire around to secure it. Cut off the shorter wire end.

12. Place the rubberized round-nose pliers at the base of this wire twist and wrap the wire around to shape it into an ear wire. Cut the wire to the desired length.

13. Using the chain-nose pliers, hold the tip of the just-curved ear wire and bend it slightly upward to finish.

14. Repeat steps 2 through 13 to make the second earring.

fig. 3   **fig. 4**   **fig. 5**

tango

These dramatic wire chandeliers will swing and move with you.

tango

Designer: Melody MacDuffee

Finished size: 2½ inches (6.4 cm) long
(not including ear wires) by ¾ inch
(1.9 cm) wide

Materials

3 feet (.91 m) of 28-gauge black
craft wire

Size 11° seed beads:
 40 red
 52 burgundy
 12 black

20 red 3-mm fire-polished beads

8 red 4-mm fire-polished beads

10 black 3-mm black bicone crystals

12 black 3-mm fire-polished beads

10 black 4-mm fire-polished beads

2 black 5 x 7-mm teardrop beads

14 black 2-inch (5 cm) head pins

1 pair of black ear wires

Tools

Wire cutters

Round-nose pliers

Chain-nose pliers

Metal file

Instructions

1. Cut the wire in half.

2. Bend the wire in half and hold the tails slightly apart, just far enough down from the bend that you can insert the top of round-nose pliers into the opening (photo 1). Give the pliers three half-twists.

fig. 1

3. Add a red seed bead, a burgundy seed bead, and another red seed bead to each wire. Twist the shortest possible section of main stem (just three or four half-twists).

4. To one tail, add a red seed, a burgundy seed, a red 3 mm fire-polished bead (FP), and another red seed. Holding the first three beads down against the main stem, use the last red seed bead to make a One-Bead Single-Leaf Motif (see box on next page) on a ⅜-inch (9.5 mm) branch (see figure 1), twisting back to the red 3 mm FP. Repeat on the other side of the earring.

fig. 2

5. Tweak these two branches so that they curve toward the beginning loop of the piece at their tips (see figure 2).

6. Add a red 4 mm FP and a black seed bead to each wire. Twist the shortest possible section of main stem.

fig. 3

7. To one wire add two red seed beads and three burgundy seed beads. Push the beads down to the main stem, and wrap the free end of the wire twice around the curved branch directly above it (see figure 3). Repeat with the other wire.

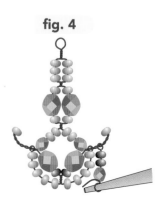

fig. 4

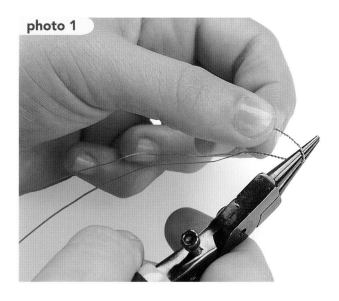

photo 1

8. To one of the wires, add two black seed beads and one red 3 mm FP (see figure 4). Make a loop by wrapping the wire all the way around the round-nose pliers, very close to the FP and then rotating the pliers 1½ times, just as you did in step 2. You may need to back the nose of the pliers out just slightly at each half-twist, since the loop will be tightening as you twist them.

9. Add another 3 mm red FP. Holding the pliers very close to it, make another wire loop. Repeat twice (see figure 5).

10. Repeat steps 8 and 9 on the other side of the earring.

11. To each wire add one 3 mm red FP. Using the two wires as one, make a wrapped loop. Finish off.

12. Repeat steps 2 through 11 for the other earring.

13. Load the head pins with the remaining beads as indicated in figure 6, and attach them to the loops.

14. Attach the top loops of the earrings to ear wires.

ONE-BEAD SINGLE-LEAF MOTIF

1. Holding the bead at the called-for distance from the main stem (⅜ inch [9.5 mm]), fold the wire back over the bead and, holding the two wires between the thumb and forefinger of your left hand, right up against the base of your bead, give the loop two or three half-twists, just enough to secure it in place.

2. Back your left hand away from the twisted portion bit by bit, still holding the two wires just slightly apart between the thumb and forefinger of your left hand as you twist the motif with your right hand. Continue until the branch is twisted all the way back to the main stem.

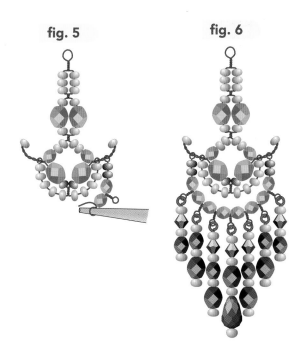

fig. 5   fig. 6

twist

A thin, spiralling wire captures a large pearl, creating the perfect earring dangle. Experiment with wire and pearl types and the number of spiral rotations used—you'll find an array of looks at your fingertips.

Designer: Jean Power

Finished size: 1³⁄₁₆ inch (20 mm)

Materials

2 cream freshwater pearls, ½-inch (1.3 cm) long oval

2 sterling silver earring findings

12-inch (30.5 cm) length of 22-gauge, sterling silver wire

Tools

Wire cutters

Ruler or measuring tape

Round-nose pliers

Chain- or flat-nose pliers

Instructions

1. Cut the wire into two 6-inch (15.2 cm) pieces. Set aside.

2. Take one of the pieces of wire and use round-nose pliers to form a ³⁄₁₆-inch (4 mm) U-shaped bend at one end. Use chain-nose pliers to squish the shape together (figure 1).

fig. 1

3. String a pearl onto the bent wire. Make a wrapped loop to secure the pearl.

fig. 2

4. Continue wrapping the wire around the top of the pearl until you have four to five coils (figure 2).

5. Make two loose spirals around the pearl to reach the bottom. Coil the remainder of the wire down the bend you made in step 2, leaving the tip of the bend exposed (figure 3). If desired, wrap the wire over itself to give the coil a heftier look. Trim any excess wire and use chain-nose pliers to tighten the wrap.

fig. 3

6. Attach an earring finding to the wrapped loop.

7. Repeat steps 2 through 6 to make a second earring.

tuscan gold

Designer: Melody MacDuffee

Finished size: 1⅞ inches (4.6 cm) long (not including ear wires) and 1 inch (2.5 cm) wide

Materials

2½ feet (76.2 cm) of 28-gauge burgundy craft wire or dead-soft wire

4 mm fire-polished beads:
    12 burgundy
    4 magenta
    8 yellow

4 mm bicone crystals:
    8 melon
    4 magenta

3 mm fire-polished beads:
    24 dark amber
    4 red

2 amber 6-mm bicone crystals

2 gold head pins

1 pair of gold ear wires

Tools

Wire cutters

Round-nose pliers

Chain-nose pliers

Metal file

With rich red and gold tones aplenty, these sultry earrings make quite a statement.

Instructions

1. Cut the wire in half.

2. Bend one of the wires in half and hold the tails slightly apart, just far enough down from the bend that you can insert the top of round-nose pliers into the opening (photo 1). Give the pliers three half-twists. This will be the top loop of the earring.

3. Add a burgundy, a magenta, and a yellow 4 mm fire-polished bead (FP) to each wire. Twist the shortest possible section of the main stem (just three or four half-twists).

4. To one of the wires, add a 4 mm melon bicone, an amber 3 mm FP, a red 3 mm FP, and another amber 3 mm FP. Holding the bicone down against the main stem, use the three FP to make a Three-Bead Single-Leaf Motif (see box below) on a ½-inch (1.3 cm) branch, twisting back to the bicone. Repeat on the other side of the earring.

5. Tweak these two branches so that they curve upward at their tips (figure 1).

6. Add a burgundy FP to each wire. Twist the shortest possible section of the main stem.

7. To one wire add a melon bicone, a magenta bicone, and a 3 mm amber FP. Push the beads down to the main stem and wrap the free end of the wire twice around the curved branch above it on the same side of the earring (figure 2). Repeat for the other side.

8. To each wire add two 3 mm amber FP, one burgundy 4 mm FP, one yellow 4 mm FP, and one amber 3 mm FP. Twist the shortest possible section of the main stem.

9. Using both wires as one, wire-wrap a loop. Clip the tails.

10. Using a head pin, add a 6 mm bicone and wire-wrap it to the bottom loop of the earring.

11. Attach the top loop of the earring to the ear wire.

12. Repeat steps 2 through 11 for the second earring.

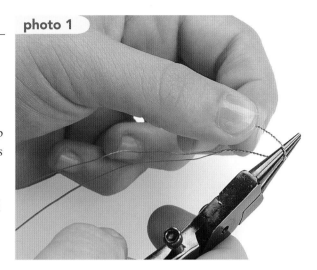

photo 1

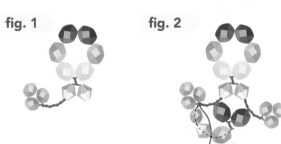

fig. 1   fig. 2

THREE-BEAD SINGLE-LEAF MOTIF

1. Slide the three beads called for in the pattern (in this instance, three FP) toward the main stem. Holding them at the called-for distance (in this case, ½ inch [1.3 cm]) from the main stem, form them into a loop with the wires crossed at the loop's base.

2. Secure the loop in place by wrapping the loose end of your working wire twice around the part between this motif and the main stem, wrapping it very tightly and right up against the base of the loop.

3. Back your left hand away from the twisted portion bit by bit, still holding your two wires just slightly apart between the thumb and forefinger of your left hand as you twist the motif with your right hand. Continue until the branch is twisted all the way back to the main stem.

turquoise twists

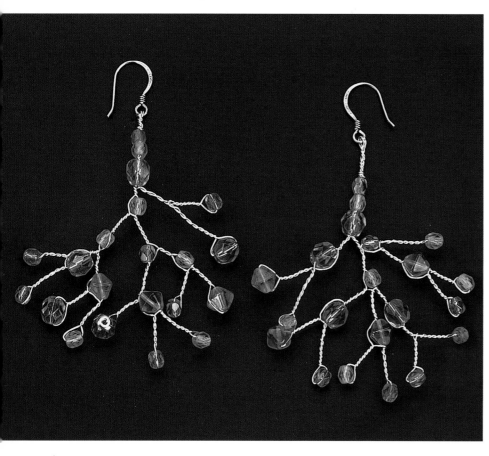

These delicate accessories feature tiny turquoise facets that shimmer on twisted silver wire.

Designer: Marinda Stewart

Finished size: 2¹⁄₂ inches (6.4 cm)

Materials

42 turquoise faceted glass beads, 4 and 6 mm diameters

26-gauge silver-colored wire, 48 inches (1.2 m) long

2 ear wires

Tools

Wire cutters

Ruler

Pliers

Instructions

1. Cut a piece of wire that's 24 inches (61 cm) long. String 19 beads of both sizes randomly on it and knot the ends so the beads stay on. Twist the wire, with beads captured in it, into a pair of opposed branches.

2. Cut off the knots at the ends of the wires. Fold the branches together in the middle and twist. Thread a 6-mm bead and a pair of 4-mm beads onto this twisted wire. Attach an ear wire to the earring using a wrapped-loop finish. Trim any excess wire.

3. Repeat steps 1 and 2 to make the second earring.

rough ruby nuggets

The designer "fell in lust" with the soft color and matte surfaces of these ruby nugget beads.

Designer: Terry Taylor

Finished size: 1¾ inches (4.4 cm)

Materials

4 rough ruby nugget beads

4 electroformed sterling silver beads

2 sterling silver beads, 1.5 mm

2 ball-end sterling silver head pins

1 pair of silver ball post earrings with ring

Tools

Wire cutter

Round-nose pliers

Needle-nose pliers

Abrasive scrub pads

Instructions

1. Use an abrasive scrubbing pad on the electroformed beads to create a matte finish on the originally shiny beads.

2. Thread the nuggets and sterling silver beads onto a head pin.

3. Using round-nose pliers, make a wrapped loop at one end of the wire.

4. Using the needle-nose pliers, open the ring of the ball-post earrings, slip the wrapped loop onto the ring, and then close the ring.

5. Repeat steps 1 through 4 to make a second earring, making sure the second earring is the same length as the first.

moon glow

What seems an elaborate wireworking technique is simply extended wraps around a beaded wire stem. The result is an earring that evokes light emanating from a full moon.

Designer: Diana Light

Finished size: 1⅛ inches (2.8 cm)

Materials

2 cream freshwater pearls,
6-mm half-round

2 semiprecious citrine saucers, 4.5 mm

2 sterling silver lever-back
earring findings

20-inch (50.8 cm) length of 24-gauge,
soft sterling wire

Tools

Flush cutters

Ruler

Chain-nose pliers

Round-nose pliers

Instructions

1. Cut 2 inches (5.1 cm) of wire. Form a simple loop ½ inch (1.3 cm) from one end. Use chain-nose pliers to bend the wire's tail so it's parallel with the long wire end (figure 1).

fig. 1

2. Slide a citrine bead onto the open end of the wire from step 1. Pull the wire end up toward the loop and make a tight coil around the loop's base. Trim any excess wire (figure 2). Set this dangle aside.

3. Cut 2 inches (5.1 cm) of wire and make a wrapped loop that attaches to one of the ear wires.

fig. 2

4. Slide a pearl onto the open end of the wire from step 1. Measure ⅝ inch (1.6 cm) down from the wrapped loop and make another wrapped loop, this time attaching it to the dangle's loop (figure 3). Set this shank aside.

5. Cut 6 inches (15.2 cm) of wire. Hold the pearl halfway up the shank and use one end of the 6-inch (15.2 cm) piece to make one wrap just above the pearl. Trim the excess tail wire.

fig. 3

6. Keep the wire as close as possible to the pearl as you bring the wire down along one side of the pearl's perimeter. Make a wrap just below the pearl by crossing over the front of the wire shank, around the back to the front, and then back up the other side of the pearl's perimeter. Make another wrap above the last wrap on top of the pearl. As with the bottom wrap, cross over the front of the shank, around back, to the front, and down the side of the pearl (figure 4).

fig. 4

7. Repeat step 6 until you reach the wrapped loops at each end of the shank. Trim the excess wire and use chain-nose pliers to squeeze the tail, tucking it beneath the coil close to the wrap.

8. Repeat the steps to make the second earring.

spring bouquet

A riot of soft color offsets pastel faceted briolettes,
creating the unmistakable look of spring.

Designer: Rachel M. Dow

Finished size: 2½ inches (6.4 cm)

Materials

2 faceted 16 x 25mm gemstone briolette drops

16 faceted 4mm glass beads in various colors

12 vintage glass flower beads:
    4 purple
    4 pink
    4 blue

4 vintage wired glass leaves

5 inches (12.7 cm) of 22-gauge dead soft, round, gold-filled wire

1½ inches (4 cm) of gold-filled 2mm chain

40 gold-filled head pins

4 rhinestone head pins

Gold-filled lever-back ear wires

Tools

Needle-nose pliers

Round-nose pliers

Wire cutters

Instructions

1. Cut the 22-gauge wire in half to make two, 2½-inch (6.4 cm) lengths. Then, cut the chain in half to make two ¾-inch (1.9 cm) lengths. Slip a briolette onto one of the lengths of wire. On one side of the bead, leave a 1-inch (2.5 cm) tail.

2. Using the needle-nose pliers, wrap the shorter end around the longer tail a few times, trimming any excess. Now use your round-nose pliers to form a small wrapped loop from the remaining wire tail, but before you wrap the wire to close the loop, attach it to an end link on one of the lengths of chain. Close the loop, complete wrapping the wire, and trim any excess.

3. String the 4mm glass beads on the gold-filled and rhinestone head pins. String the vintage flower beads on the gold-filled head pins only. Use the needle-nose and round-nose pliers to make wrapped loops at the end of each head pin for attaching the beads to the chain. Begin attaching the beads to the links closest to the briolette and work your way up the chain.

4. Attach the wired leaves, two per earring, close to the briolette. Add more beads to the bottom of the chain, gradually adding less as you get to the top. Randomly place two of the rhinestone head pins with beads on each earring.

5. Repeat the steps to make the second earring, then attach the lever-back ear wires to each.

confetti hoops

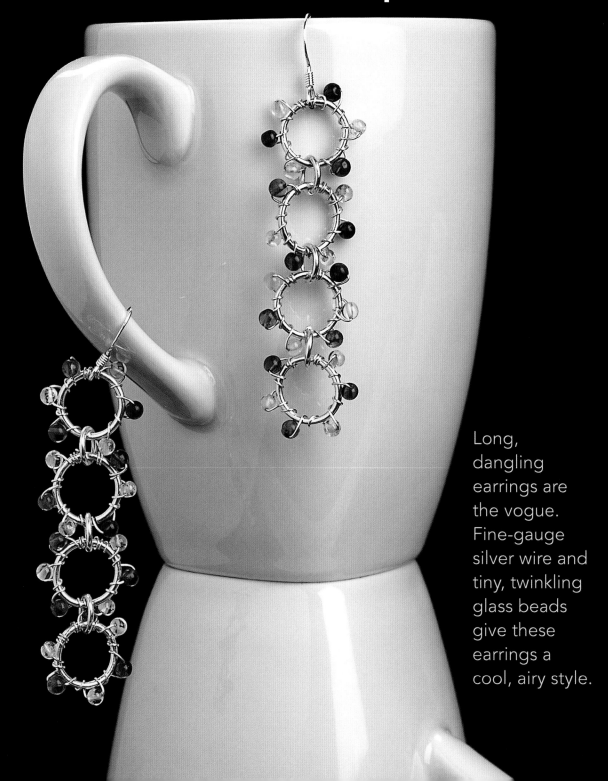

Long, dangling earrings are the vogue. Fine-gauge silver wire and tiny, twinkling glass beads give these earrings a cool, airy style.

Materials

Designer: Rachel M. Dow

Finished size: 2 inches (5.1 cm)

48 gemstone beads in various colors, 3 to 4 mm diameter

26-gauge dead-soft sterling silver wire, 4 feet (1.2 m) long

8 jump rings, 16-gauge sterling silver, 10 mm diameter

6 jump rings, 18-gauge sterling silver, 6 mm diameter

2 sterling silver ear wires

Tools

Wire cutters

Ruler

Chain-nose pliers

Flat-nose pliers

Instructions

1. Using flush cutters, cut four pieces of 26-gauge wire, each 5¼ inches (13.3 cm) long.

2. Wrap one piece of 26-gauge wire twice around a 10-mm jump ring to secure it; using chain-nose pliers to grasp the thinner wire will help you get a tight wrap. Add a bead to the wire, hold it in place on the outer edge of the 10-mm jump ring, and wrap the wire tightly around the jump ring twice, being careful not to kink the light wire as you work.

3. Add another bead to the wire and continue wrapping and adding beads, working your way around the jump ring until you've attached six evenly spaced beads to it. Secure the tail of the wire by wrapping it tightly twice around the jump ring, close to the point where you began the wrapping. Cut off any extra wire.

4. Repeat steps 2 and 3 to make a total of four bead-wrapped 10-mm jump rings.

5. Use a fingernail or the tip of the chain-nose pliers to separate the beginning/end wraps of wire on one of the bead-wrapped jump rings, and attach an ear wire there.

6. Using three 6-mm jump rings, link three more bead-wrapped jump rings sequentially to the one with the ear wire.

7. Repeat the steps to make a second earring.

dancing branches

Capture the appearance of buds on bare branches in springtime with these delicate earrings.

Instructions

1. Use wire cutters to flush trim the tip of the wire. Use chain-nose pliers to grasp the trimmed end and fold the tip of the wire back on itself. Squeeze the fold flat so it's flush.

2. Thread the beads that you want to use for the longest branch onto the wire. Use chain-nose pliers to bend the wire at a 90-degree angle, about 1½ inches (3.8 cm) from the folded tip. Use wire cutters to flush cut the wire to loop length and round-nose pliers to form a simple loop.

3. Repeat steps 1 and 2 to create the longest branch for the other earring. The two branches need to be the same length for visual balance but otherwise don't need to match.

4. Make two more branches for each earring in the same manner. Add one or two beads to each branch, but don't make exact matches. These branches can vary in length but should be shorter than the first branch.

5. When all the branches are finished, space out the beads as desired by using chain-nose plierse to bend kinks in the wire.

6. Use flat-nose pliers to open a loop on one of the earring findings, just as you would open a jump ring. Add one of the longest branches and two of the shorter branches in any order you desire. Close the loop. Repeat with the other earring finding.

Designer: Kathy Frey

Finished size: 1¾ inches (4.4 cm)

Materials

26-, 24-, or 22-gauge half-hard sterling silver wire (use the gauge that best fits your beads), 8 inches (20.3 cm)

Selection of semiprecious stone, glass, and/or pearl beads

French ear wires or posts with hanging loops

Tools

Wire cutters

Chain-nose pliers

Ruler

Round-nose pliers

Flat-nose pliers

Designer's Tip

This set is easy to customize by choosing different color palettes for the stones. Have fun playing with colors and stone shapes for your own special look.

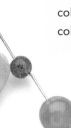

bollywood dreams

Carnelian beads and gold wire combine to create exotic
earrings reminiscent of the wares of Far Eastern markets.
The designer's fine wirework has the appearance of filigree.

Designer: Eni Oken

Finished size: 2¼ inches (5.7 cm)

Materials

12 round beads, 7 mm diameter

2 top-drilled faceted flat pear car-nelian beads,* ½ inch (1.3 cm) long

20 round carnelian seed beads, 3 mm diameter

2 round carnelian beads, 5 mm diameter

26-gauge gold-filled dead-soft wire, 9 feet (2.7 m) long, for the wraps

18-gauge gold-filled dead-soft wire, 7½ inches (19 cm) long, for the teardrop-shaped element

2 gold-filled lever-back ear wires

Tools

Wire cutters

Ruler

Round-nose pliers

Flat-nose pliers

Wooden dowel or pen, ¾ inch (1.9 cm) diameter

Mallet or hammer

Anvil

*Faceted flat pear beads are sometimes called briolettes.

Instructions

1. Cut 6 pieces of 26-gauge wire, each 3 inches (7.6 cm) long. Make eye pins with tiny wrapped loops out of each of them, then slip a 7-mm round bead onto each. Close the open ends with another miniscule wrapped loop. Cut off any excess wire.

2. Cut the 18-gauge wire in half. Working with one piece, form small loops at both ends of it. Using the wooden dowel and your fingers, form the wire into a teardrop shape. Flatten the shape on an anvil with a mallet or hammer until it's work-hardened.

3. To create the flat-pear dangles at the earring's center, cut a piece of 26-gauge wire, 3 inches (7.6 cm) long. Place a flat pear on it, leaving a tail 1 inch (2.5 cm) long on one side; wrap the shorter wire around the longer one several times. Trim the short end of the wire. Next, use round-nose pliers to form a small wrapped loop from the remaining wire, making the loop as close as possible to the wrapping you just did and winding some of the excess wire on top of the existing wrapping. Trim the wire closely.

4. To assemble all the elements, cut a piece of 26-gauge wire 2½ feet (76.2 cm) long. Leaving a 1-inch-long (2.5 cm) tail to help you hold onto it, start at one of the loops on the teardrop shape and tightly coil the wire to one of the loops for ¼ inch (0.6 cm); trim the tail. Slip a seed bead onto the working wire, making sure the bead is positioned at the outermost edge of the wire teardrop, and continue coiling another ³⁄₁₆ inch (0.5 cm). Add another seed bead to the working wire and coil another ³⁄₁₆ inch (0.5 cm). Now slip a seed bead and one of the dangles you made in step 1 onto the working wire. Continue to wrap the wire and add the seed beads and dangles in this way until you've attached them all. After you finish, if the beads aren't symmetrically spaced on the teardrop, spread out the coils a bit until they are.

5. Bring together the two loops of the teardrop element so that one is atop the other, then wrap them together twice tightly. Form a small cap by wrapping the shoulders of the teardrop, below the loops, six more times. On the last wrap, slip the flat pear dangle onto the working wire, then use round-nose pliers to twist a small wrapped loop that faces into the center of the teardrop shape. Finish by tightly coiling it around the teardrop wire, near the cap. Trim any excess wire.

6. Using a 3-inch (7.6 cm) length of 26-gauge wire and a 5-mm bead, make a wrapped bead loop link that connects one of its loops to the two joined loops above the cap, and the other one in an ear wire.

7. Repeat the steps to make a second earring.

pink on pink

Pink opaque stones are rare in the gem world. The small heishi pearls both mirror and soften the organic texture of the nuggets.

Designer: Thomas Jay Parker

Finished size: 1½ inches (3.8 cm)

Materials

2 small pink opal nuggets

6 natural top-drilled pink heishi pearls

8 silver 2½-inch (6.4 cm) head pins

2 lengths of silver chain, each ¾ inch (1.9 cm) long

2 silver French ear wires

Tools

Flat-nose pliers

Round-nose pliers

Wire cutters

Instructions

1. String a pink opal onto a head pin. Using the round-nose pliers, make the loop for a wrapped loop, attach one end of a length of chain to it, then use the flat-nose pliers to hold the loop while you wrap the tail around the wire. Trim any excess wire.

2. String three heishi pearls on three separate head pins. Using wrapped loops, attach them where desired on the length of chain. Attach the ear wire to the middle of the length of chain, allowing the chain to drape and the pearls to dangle.

3. Repeat the steps to make the other earring.

good earth

Be one with both beauty and style in a combination of coral, bone, and antiqued brass.

Designer: Candie Cooper

Finished size: 1¼ inches (3.2 cm) long

Materials

18 green seed beads

2 round coral beads, 4 mm

2 brass head pins

4 brass spacer beads, 5 mm

2 faux bone round beads, 10 mm

2 ear wires

Tools

Flat-nose pliers

Scissors

Round-nose pliers

Wire cutters

Instructions

1. To make the first earring, thread the following onto one of the head pins: one seed bead, one 5-mm spacer bead, one faux bone round bead, one 5-mm spacer bead, two seed beads, one coral bead, and six seed beads. Use the round-nose pliers to make a small loop just above the last seed bead, and trim any excess with the wire cutters. Add one of the earring wires to the loop, and use the flat-nose pliers to firmly close the loop.

2. Repeat step 1 to make the second earring.

Designer's Tip

You can age your brass findings by holding them in an open flame for a few seconds, and then quenching them in cold water.

hoopla

When the compliments fly at you from right and left,
you won't have to tell anyone how easy these were to make.

Designer: Anjanette Randolph

Finished size: 2¾ inches (7 cm) long

Materials

Round brass wire, 24 gauge,
5 feet (1.5 m)

30 lapis lazuli round beads, 4 mm

2 gold-plated jump rings, 7 mm

2 gold-plated ear wires

Tools

Ruler

Side-cutting pliers

Round-nose pliers

Flat-nose pliers

Instructions

1. Using side-cutting pliers, cut six pieces of brass wire, each 9 inches (22.9 cm) long.

2. Hold three of the wire pieces side by side so that you can bend them simultaneously. Use round-nose pliers to create a loop in the gathered wires, about 1 inch (2.5 cm) from one end. Wrap the tail around the loop, and clip off the excess wire. Use flat-nose pliers to bend the edges into a neatly formed, wrapped loop.

3. Slide 15 lapis beads onto the middle wire. Using round-nose pliers, make another wrapped loop at the other end of the three wires.

4. Use chain-nose pliers to open a jump ring. Slide both wrapped loops onto the jump ring to form a teardrop shape. Slip an ear wire onto the jump ring, and close the jump ring.

5. Repeat steps 2 through 4 to make the second earring.

lantern

The carved amethyst beads and golden fringes of these super-simple earrings evoke swaying paper lanterns of the Orient.

Designer: Kate Drew-Wilkinson

Finished size: 3½ inches (8.9 cm)

Materials

4 round beads, 14-karat gold filled, 2.5 mm diameter

8 spacers, 14-karat gold filled, 2.5 mm diameter

4 turquoise beads, 6 mm diameter

4 spacers, 14-karat gold filled, 4 mm diameter

2 carved amethyst oval beads, 10 x 15 mm

4 round beads, 14-karat gold filled, 2 mm diameter

2 turquoise beads, 4 mm diameter

22-gauge half-hard 14-karat gold-filled wire, 9 inches (22.9 cm) long

14-karat gold-filled 1 mm flat chain, 16 inches (40.6 cm) long

2 gold jump rings, 5 mm diameter

2 14-karat gold-filled ear wires

Tools

Wire cutters

Ruler

Round-nose pliers

Flat-nose pliers

Instructions

1. Cut six segments of chain that range in length from ¾ to 1¾ inches (1.9 to 4.4 cm).

2. Cut a piece of wire 3 inches (7.6 cm) long. Fashion it into a wrapped bead loop link, attaching one end of all the pieces of chain in one loop and stringing beads onto it in the following sequence: 2.5-mm round, 2.5-mm spacer, 6-mm turquoise, 4-mm spacer, amethyst, 4-mm spacer, 6-mm turquoise, 2.5-mm spacer, and 2.5-mm round. Cut off any extra wire.

3. Cut a piece of wire 1½ inches (3.8 cm) long. Make a wrapped bead loop link with beads in the following sequence: 2-mm round, 2.5-mm spacer, 4-mm turquoise, 2.5-mm spacer, and 2-mm round. Trim off the extra wire.

4. Attach the two bead links to each other with a jump ring. Connect the ear wire to the shorter bead link.

5. Repeat the steps to make a second earring.

waterfall

Sparkling gems in varying shapes
tumble from simple ear wires.

Designer: Tamara Honaman

Finished size: 4 inches (10.2 cm)

Materials

Citrine oval, 8 mm

Trillion amethyst triangular, 8 mm

Pear peacock topaz, 8 mm

2 coin charms, 20 mm

Oval stone setting, 8 mm

Pear stone setting, 8 mm

Triangular stone setting, 8 mm

6 sterling silver jump rings, 5 mm

4 sterling silver jump rings, 4 mm

2 sterling silver French ear wires
with bead

18-inch (45.7 cm) length of 24-gauge
sterling silver wire

10-inch (25.4 cm) length of 1.5 mm fine
sterling silver rolo chain

Tools

Chain-nose pliers, 2 pair

Round-nose pliers

Wire cutters

Instructions

1. Cut the silver chain into five sections, varying the lengths from ¾ to 1½ inches (1.9 to 3.8 cm).

2. Place a faceted stone, face down, on a flat surface. Place the setting, also face down, on top of the stone. Press down on the setting until you feel the stone click into it. Ensure that the stone is secure; if it's not, you can try to adjust using a toothpick or remove it and try again. If the prongs don't seem to want to let the stone in, you could use the chain-nose pliers to adjust one prong open to allow the stone to be gripped in place. However, the settings are calibrated and typically are ready for setting!

3. Using the chain-nose pliers, gently squeeze the prongs on both sides of the stone to only slightly move them (figure 1), working your way around the setting until the stone is secure and all of the prongs are against the stone.

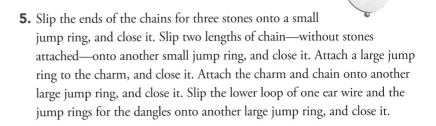

fig. 1

fig. 2

4. Cut a 3-inch (7.6 cm) length of wire. Place your round-nose pliers in the center of the cut length of wire. Begin a wrapped loop but, before wrapping, slip the top of the setting onto the wire. Continue with the wrapped loop, capturing the setting inside it (figure 2). Make another wrapped loop with the remaining section of wire, capturing the last link of one length of chain. Seat the remaining stones in their settings and secure a wrapped loop wire to each one, while attaching a length of chain.

5. Slip the ends of the chains for three stones onto a small jump ring, and close it. Slip two lengths of chain—without stones attached—onto another small jump ring, and close it. Attach a large jump ring to the charm, and close it. Attach the charm and chain onto another large jump ring, and close it. Slip the lower loop of one ear wire and the jump rings for the dangles onto another large jump ring, and close it.

6. Repeat the steps to make the other earring.

Designer's Tips

● You know a stone is seated properly in a setting when you can look across the surface of the stone and it reflects the light on an even plane and, if you run your finger across the surface, the stone doesn't budge.
● The set stones are attached to the chain with a double-wrapped loop. This requires more wire than a basic wire-wrap because one loop captures the setting and another connects to a link in the chain.

pastel flower
chandelier

Fresh and flirty, these alluring flower earrings are sure to turn heads.

Designer: Melody MacDuffee

Finished size: 1⅞ inches (4.7 cm) long, not including ear wires

Materials

7 feet (2.13 m) of 28-gauge silver craft wire or dead-soft sterling silver wire

12 blue 4-mm bicone crystal beads

2- to 3-mm round gemstone beads or size 11° seed beads:

    34 green (chalcedony)

    16 yellow (jade)

    4 turquoise

1 pair of gold ear wires

2 gold 6-mm soldered rings, or extender chain

2 yellow 6-mm bicone crystal beads

2 gold head pins

Tools

Wire cutters

Round-nose pliers

Chain-nose pliers

Metal file

Instructions

1. Cut the wire into two 16-inch (40.6 cm) and two 26-inch (66 cm) pieces.

2. Using one of the 16-inch (40.6 cm) pieces of wire, add six blue bicones to the wire and slide them down to its center point. (**Note:** From this point on, the wires on either side of your beads will be referred to as two separate wires.) Form the beads into a loop, with the wires crossed at its base. Secure the loop in place by wrapping one of the wires (this will be the working wire) around the other (now the dormant wire) twice, very tightly, right up against the base of the loop. Bring the working wire all the way under the loop and then back over, across the front of it. Using either one of the wires, make a Six-Petal Flower Motif (see box below) to lie across the ring of bicones, tacking it to the bottom-center point of the bicone ring just before you add the center bead (figure 1).

fig. 1

SIX-PETAL FLOWER MOTIF

The finished motif in an alternate colorway.

1. Add six green rounds (these are the "petals") to your wire and slide them down to its center point. Form the beads into a loop with the wires crossed at its base. Secure the loop in place by wrapping the working wire around the dormant wire twice, very tightly, right up against the base of the loop.

2. Bring the working wire all the way under the loop and then back over, across the front of it. Add a yellow round and position it in the center of the loop.

3. Holding the two wires between the thumb and forefinger of your left hand, right up against the base of your loop, give the loop two or three half-twists, just enough to secure it in place.

4. Back your left hand away from this twisted portion bit by bit, still holding the two wires just slightly apart, between the thumb and forefinger of your left hand, as you twist the motif with your right hand, thus beginning the main stem.

FIVE-PETAL FLOWER MOTIF

1. Add five green rounds (these are the "petals") to the wire and slide them down to its center point. Form the beads into a loop with the wires crossed at its base. Secure the loop in place by wrapping one of the wires (the working wire) around the other (now the dormant wire) twice, very tightly, right up against the base of the loop.

2. Bring the working wire all the way under the loop and then back over, across the front of it.

3. Twist a ⅛-inch (3 mm) length of main stem. Using round-nose pliers and both wires, make a wrapped loop at the end of the stem, coiling the wires back down as close as possible to the motif.

4. Bring the wires behind the motif, going past two bicones (see figure 2). Bring the wires around and through, between the second and third petals, and pull them tight. Twist a ⅛-inch (3 mm) length of stem.

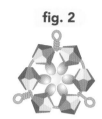

fig. 2

5. Repeat steps 3 and 4.

6. Repeat step 3 again. Finish off the wires.

7. Curve the first and third wire-wrapped loops downward somewhat.

8. Attach an ear wire to the second wire-wrapped loop made, making sure that the flower faces forward.

9. Repeat steps 2 through 8 for the other earring.

10. Using one of the 26-inch (66 cm) pieces of wire, and using green rounds for the petals, make a Five-Petal Flower Motif (see box above) at the wire's center point.

11. Twist a ⅛-inch (3 mm) length of main stem. Using round-nose pliers and both wires, wire-wrap a loop at the end of the stem, coiling the wires back down as close as possible to the motif.

12. Add a yellow round to one of the wires, and carry it across the front of the flower to serve as the flower's center. Carry the unbeaded wire across, behind the flower to meet the first. Twist the shortest possible length of main stem (see figure 3).

fig. 3

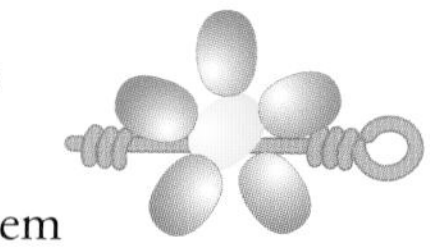

13. Using yellow rounds for the petals, instead of green ones, make a Five-Petal Flower Motif at the wire's center point.

14. Add a turquoise round to one of the wires, and carry it across the front of the flower to serve as the flower's center. (Be sure that three of the yellow round beads lie above the wire and two below.) Carry the unbeaded wire across, behind the flower to meet the first. Twist the shortest possible length of main stem (see figure 4).

15. Using green rounds for the petals, make a Five-Petal Flower.

16. Add a yellow round bead to one of the wires, and carry it across the front of the flower to serve as the flower's center. Carry the unbeaded wire across, behind the flower to meet the first. Twist a ⅛-inch (3 mm) length of main stem. Using round-nose pliers and both wires, wire-wrap a loop at the end of the stem, coiling your wires back down as close as possible to the motif (see figure 5). Finish off.

17. Using a scrap of wire, insert it between the bottom two yellow rounds, and wrap it around the wire there several times to anchor it in place (see figure 5 again). Twist a ⅛-inch (3 mm) length of stem, and wire-wrap a loop, coiling your wires back down as close as possible to the motif. Finish off.

18. Repeat steps 10 through 17 for the other earring.

19. Use the jump rings to attach the earring tops to the bottom strips of flowers.

20. Add a turquoise round, a 6 mm bicone, and a green round to one of the head pins. Wire-wrap it to the bottom center loop.

21. Repeat step 20 for the other earring.

fig. 4

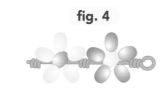

fig. 5

The dynamic spiral shape and brightly colored beads of these earrings are sure to attract attention at parties, or simply enhance an upbeat mood.

spiral lights

Designer: Rachel M. Dow

Finished size: 1⅝ inches (4.1 cm)

Materials

10 pairs of round or button-shaped freshwater pearl beads in various colors, 4 mm diameter

2 pieces of 18-gauge colored wire, each 6½ inches (16.5 cm) long, for the armature

2 pieces of 26-gauge dead-soft gold-filled wire, each 10¼ inches (26 cm) long, for the wrap

2 gold-tone ear wires

Tools

Round-nose pliers

Flat-nose pliers

Wire cutters

Instructions

Note: Match the sizes, shapes, and color patterns of the beads.

1. Straighten out the 18-gauge wire. Make a closed loop at the end of the wire. Grasp the loop with the widest part of a pair of chain-nose pliers and, holding your pliers hand stationary, rotate the wire into a loose spiral shape, leaving ½ inch (1.3 cm) of the tail end of the wire remaining.

2. With the remaining tail end of the wire, make another loop in the opposite direction of the spiral. As you work, align it with the loop at the spiral's center. Trim any extra length of the wire that's left.

3. Secure the 26-gauge wire around the center loop in the spiral, slip on a bead, and tuck it into the spiral's loop. Hold the bead in place and wrap the wire twice around the spiral.

4. Add nine more beads, leaving a little bit of spacing between each one. As you work, make sure that your wrapping is tight and that the beads are snug against the spiral without distorting its shape. Straighten any kinks with chain-nose pliers. Finish by tightly wrapping the lighter wire three times around the base of the spiral's outer loop. Snip off any extra wire. When you wrap the second spiral, make a mirror-image earring by working on the opposite side and in the opposite direction as the first one.

5. Attach the gold-tone ear wires to the earrings' exterior loops.

6. Repeat the steps to make the second earring.

nefertiti

These elegant earrings are worthy embellishments for a queen of the Nile. You can make a more understated version by making just one ring of pearls instead of four.

Designer: Sharon Bateman

Finished size: 1⅜ inches (3.4 cm)

Materials

48 freshwater pearls, 5-mm rice

48 gold-filled, 26-gauge headpins, 1 inch (2.5 cm) long

8 gold-filled, 8-mm jump rings (or make your own from 5 inches [12.7 cm] of gold-filled 20-gauge wire)

2 gold-filled earring findings

Tools

2 sets of chain-nose pliers

Round-nose pliers

Flush cutters, optional

¼-inch (6 mm) dowel, 4 inches (10.2 cm) long, optional

Metal file or emery board, optional

Instructions

1. Slide one pearl onto a headpin. Make a wrapped loop to secure the pearl. Repeat to make 48 pearl dangles in all. Set aside.

2. If desired, make your own jump rings.

3. Use the chain-nose pliers to open a jump ring. Slide on six pearl dangles and an earring finding. Close the jump ring.

4. Open a jump ring and slip six pearl dangles onto it. Before closing the jump ring, attach it to the jump ring from the previous step (figure 1).

fig. 1

5. Repeat step 4 until you've connected four pearl dangle-embellished jump rings.

6. Repeat the steps to make a second earring.

green turquoise spikes

We think you get the point—these are great earrings. They're delicate yet edgy, daring, and fun. The colors would brighten basic black, but the design would pair well with a sundress and sandals.

Designer: Nancy Kugel

Finished size: 3 inches (7.6 cm)

Materials

2 green turquoise spikes

2 extra-long silver head pins

12 garnet seed beads

6 garnet rounds, 4mm

2 turquoise rounds, 8 mm

1 pair of ear wires

Tools

Wire cutters

Round-nose pliers

Instructions

1. Thread a spike on an extra-long head pin. Cut off the stop. Using the round-nose pliers, make a wrapped loop for attaching the spike to the ear wire.

2. Cut the stop off a head pin and string on three garnet seed beads, an 8mm turquoise round, and three more seed beads. Make wrapped loops on both ends of the wire, and attach them to the wire sides of the wrapped loop you made for the spike.

3. Thread three 4mm garnet beads on three separate head pins. Make wrapped loops on the ends of each. Attach them to the wrapped loop at the top of the spike.

4. Repeat the steps to make the second earring.

fiesta

Beads in an energetic color combination give the impression you're wearing a party!

Designer: Kate Drew-Wilkinson

Finished size: 3³/₈ inches (8.6 cm)

Materials

20 sterling silver round beads, 2.5 mm diameter

20 copper heishi spacer beads

8 red ceramic donut beads, ½ inch (1.3 cm) diameter

6 turquoise ceramic beads, 8 mm diameter

20-gauge half-hard silver wire, 2 feet (61 cm)

2 ear wires

Tools

Wire cutters

Ruler

Round-nose pliers

Flat-nose pliers

Instructions

1. Cut the wire into 3-inch (7.6 cm) pieces.

2. Make two wrapped bead loop links, threading a sterling silver bead, three spacers, and another sterling silver bead on each; slip an ear wire on one loop end and a donut on the other. Keep one of the loops large enough to allow the donut free movement.

3. Make another wrapped bead loop link with a sterling silver bead, a spacer, and another sterling silver bead threaded on it, attaching one loop to the donut from the previous step and leaving the other loop empty.

4. Using one piece of wire, make a wrapped bead loop link with a sterling silver bead, a spacer, a round ceramic bead, another spacer, and another sterling silver bead on it. Slip a donut on a loop before closing it. Keep the loops large enough to allow the donut free movement. Before closing the loops, attach a donut to one of them, then link the other loop to the empty end of the link from the previous step. Repeat two more times.

5. Repeat the steps to make a second earring.

The tiny crystals on these shimmery earrings capture and refract light.
Wear these with a white shirt and jeans and let them draw all eyes to you.

Designer: Cynthia Deis

Finished size: 2½ inches (6.7 cm)

Materials

14 gold-plated filigree teardrops,
15 x 20 mm

36 clear AB crystal bicone beads, 2 mm

22 gold-filled head pins, 1 inch (2.5 cm)

1 pair of gold-filled 24-gauge ear wires

Gold-filled 24-gauge wire,
6 inches (15.2 cm)

Tools

Chain-nose pliers

Round-nose pliers

Wire cutters

Instructions

1. Slide one bead onto a head pin and form a simple loop to secure it. *Note:* It may help to very gently grasp the crystal with chain-nose pliers while turning the loop with round-nose pliers. Repeat to make 11 dangles in all. Set aside.

2. Cut a 1-inch (2.5 cm) length of wire. Form a simple loop at one end. Slide on one bead and form a simple loop to secure it. Repeat to make six bead links in all. Set aside.

3. Use your fingers to shape one of the ear wires until it's a smooth curve. Slide on one bead and use your fingers to reshape the ear wire.

4. Lay the teardrops, faceup, in three rows: one in row 1, three in row 2, and three in row 3.

fig. 1

row 1

row 2

row 3

5. Attach the ear wire to the top of the row 1 teardrop. Use a bead link to connect the top of the first row 2 teardrop to the bottom left hole of the row 1 teardrop; a link to connect the top of the second row 2 teardrop to the bottom center hole of the row 1 teardrop; and a third link to connect the top of the third row 2 teardrop to the bottom right hole of the row 1 teardrop. Use bead links to connect the top of each row 3 teardrop to the bottom center hole of each row 2 teardrop (figure 1).

fig. 2

6. Add one dangle to each of the three holes at the bottom of the row 3 teardrops. Connect one dangle to the bottom left hole of the first row 1 teardrop, and one to the bottom right hole of the third row 1 tear drop (figure 2).

7. Repeat the steps to make a second earring.

whisper drops

These delicate, lightweight earrings can dress up or dress down. Whatever the occasion, their design will be to your jewelry box what a black dress is to your wardrobe.

Designer: Ellen Gerritse

Finished size: 2½ inches (6.4 cm)

Materials

18 sterling silver seed beads

18 white-frost twisted tube beads, 12 mm long

18 sterling silver crimp beads

18 sterling silver eye pins, 1 inch (2.5 cm) long

2 sterling silver ear wires

Tools

Crimping pliers

Pliers

Instructions

1. Slip one eye pin onto another eye pin, then a seed bead, a tube bead, and a crimp bead. Close the crimp bead onto the beaded eye pin, ½ inch (1.3 cm) from the end.

2. Add another eye pin to the element you made in step 1, with the same sequence of beads and ending in a crimp bead.

3. Repeat steps 1 and 2 to make two more beaded elements.

4. Hang all three elements on an ear wire loop.

5. Repeat the steps to make a second earring.

ivy

These earrings are like delicate vines mingling with the tendrils of your hair.

Designer: Terry Taylor	
Finished size: 3 inches (7.6 cm)	

Materials

10 leaf-shaped beads, 19 mm

12 sterling silver jump rings, 6 mm

2 sterling silver ear studs (ball with drop), 6 mm

2½-inch (6.4 cm) length of 1.5 mm sterling silver chain

Tools

Chain-nose pliers, 2 pair

Round-nose pliers

Wire cutters

Instructions

1. Cut the chain in half. Set one piece aside for the second earring.

2. Open all of the jump rings, and slide a leaf-shaped bead onto each one. Slip the last link of the chain onto one of the jump rings, and close it. Attach four more leaves with jump rings, evenly spaced, along the length of the chain. Place the uppermost bead just a link or two from the top of the chain.

3. Slip another jump ring onto the top link of the embellished chain, and then through the loop at the bottom of the ear stud (figure 1).

4. Repeat steps 2 and 3 to make a second earring.

fig. 1

coral blossom

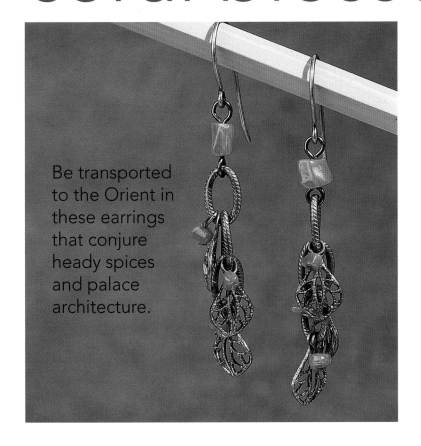

Be transported to the Orient in these earrings that conjure heady spices and palace architecture.

Designer: Cynthia Deis

Finished size: 2 inches (5.1 cm)

Materials

6 natural brass filigree leaves, 8 mm

2 red branch coral nugget beads, 6 mm

6 red branch coral nugget beads, 2 mm

6 natural brass head pins, 1 inch (2.5 cm)

6 oval natural brass decorative jump rings, 6 x 10 mm

2 antiqued brass ear wires

Gunmetal 20-gauge wire, 2 inches (5.1 cm)

Tools

Wire cutters

Chain-nose pliers

Round-nose pliers

Instructions

1. Slide one 2-mm bead onto a head pin. Form a simple loop to secure the bead. Repeat twice. Set the bead dangles aside.

2. Cut a 1-inch (2.5 mm) length of wire and form a simple loop at one end. Slip on one 6-mm bead and form another simple loop to secure the bead link.

3. Connect one end of one of the bead links to an ear wire. Set aside.

4. Open a decorative jump ring and slide on one filigree leaf and one bead dangle. Close the ring. Open a second ring, slide on one filigree leaf, one bead dangle, and the first ring. Close the ring. Open a third ring, slide on one filigree leaf, one bead dangle, and the second ring. Close the ring (figure 1).

    fig. 1

5. Connect one end of the embellished chain made in the previous step to the open end of the bead link.

6. Repeat the steps to make the second earring.

cleopatra

The intriguing qualities of green onyx and chrysoprase are displayed to perfection in this simple yet stylish earring design.

Designer: Valérie MacCarthy

Finished size: 1½ inches (3.8 cm)

Materials

2 green onyx briolettes, 12 mm

2 chrysoprase briolettes, 6 mm

2 gold-filled ball-post earrings with open rings

12-inch (30.5 cm) length of 24-gauge gold-filled wire

4-inch (10.2 cm) length of 26-gauge gold-filled wire

Tools

Chain-nose pliers

Round-nose pliers

Wire cutters

Large rubberized round-nose pliers

Ruler

fig. 1

fig. 2

fig. 3

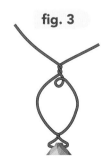

Instructions

1. With wire cutters, cut the 12-inch (30.5 cm) length of 24-gauge wire into two 6-inch (15.2 cm) segments.

2. Select one of the wires and slide a 12-mm green onyx briolette onto the middle of it. Bend the wires on both sides of the bead until they cross, and then twist them around once to secure the briolette in place.

3. Using the large rubberized round-nose pliers, bend both wires into a curve (figure 1). Before continuing, make sure the wires are curved to a pleasing size to accommodate the 6-mm chrysoprase briolette; hold it in the middle of the curve to check. Adjust the size of the curve as necessary.

4. Keeping the wires crossed and using the round-nose pliers, grasp one wire on the inside of the cross and loop it around (figure 2).

5. With the chain-nose pliers, hold both the loop you've just made and the opposite wire and twist them around just above the loop (figure 3). Cut off one wire above the twist.

6. Loop the remaining wire around and slide the ring of the ball-post earring onto the wire.

7. Hold this loop with the chain-nose pliers and wrap the wire around the twist you made in step 5. Cut off the excess wire.

8. Cut the 4-inch (10.2 cm) length of 26-gauge wire in half, making two 2-inch (5.1 cm) lengths. Slide a 6-mm chrysoprase briolette onto one wire about ¾ inch (1.9 cm) from the end. Bend both ends up until the wires are crossing.

9. Twist the wires around one and one-half times and cut off the shorter wire end. Adjust the remaining wire so that it is facing forward (not to the side).

10. Using the round-nose pliers, loop this wire and slide it through the bottom loop you created on the earring.

11. After one loop is hanging from the other, use the chain-nose pliers to hold this new loop and wrap the wire around the twist you made in step 9. Cut off the excess wire.

12. Repeat the steps to make the second earring.

florentine lace

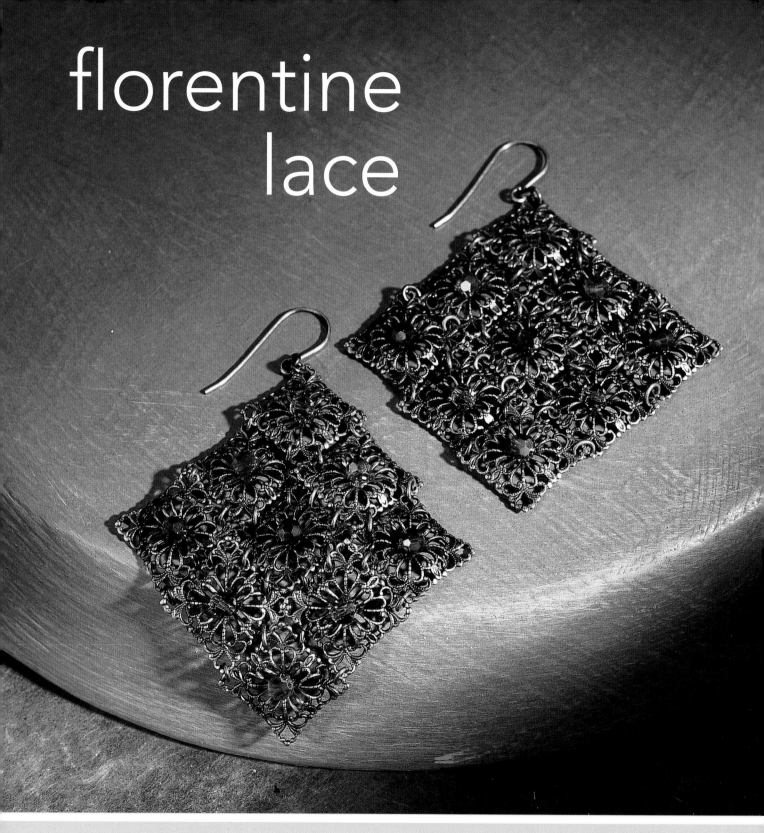

Have you received an invite to a masquerade ball held in an Italian Renaissance *palazzo*? These delicate earrings would be just the thing to flaunt. Or if you prefer, make a single square to dangle as a pendant from a velvet ribbon.

Designer: Cynthia Deis

Finished size: 2½ inches (6.3 cm)

Materials

18 antiqued brass square filigree pieces, 15 mm

4 mm crystal round beads:
    6 green
    6 pink
    6 blue

52 antiqued brass oval jump rings, 3 x 4 mm

1 pair of antiqued brass ear wires

Medium-width flexible beading wire, 36 inches (91.4 cm)

Tools

Chain-nose pliers

Round-nose pliers

Wire cutters

Instructions

1. Lay out nine filigree squares in three rows of three to make one larger square.

2. Following the positions marked in figure 1, use jump rings to connect the squares. Check that the front of each filigree piece faces forward.

3. Cut one 2-inch (5.1 cm) length of wire and string on one green crystal bead. Starting with a corner filigree square, and working from the front center of that square, push both wire ends through the filigree holes. Tie a secure square knot. Trim the wire ends close to the knot. Repeat with all the filigree squares, following figure 2 for bead color placement. Take care to pass the wires through each square at the same angle so all the bead holes are parallel.

4. Connect a jump ring to the open hole of the corner green filigree square. Use another jump ring to attach the ring just placed to an ear wire (figure 2).

5. Repeat the steps to make the second earring.

fig. 1

fig. 2

hearts

Delicate charms and crystals command attention when grouped along dainty chains.

Designer: Marlynn McNutt

Finished size: 2¾ inches (7 cm)

Materials

14 light rose bicone crystals, 4 mm

8 mauve freshwater pearls (potato), 8 mm

2 sterling silver Celtic filigree charms, 6 mm

8 sterling silver flat heart charms, 5 mm

4 sterling silver puff heart charms, 8 mm

2 sterling silver decorative heart charms, 11 mm

2 sterling silver smooth, flat heart drops, 10 mm

22 sterling silver head pins, 2 inches (5 cm) long

2 sterling silver ear hoops with 3 loops, 15 mm

24 sterling silver jump rings, 3 mm

7-inch (17.8 cm) length of 2 mm sterling silver rolo chain

Tools

Chain-nose pliers, 2 pair

Round-nose pliers

Flush wire cutters

Instructions

1. Cut four pieces of chain 1 inch (2.5 cm) long and two pieces of chain 1⅜ inches (3.5 cm) long.

2. Run a head pin through a bicone, and finish with a simple loop. Add a head pin with a simple loop to the remaining bicones and pearls in the same manner.

3. Open the jump rings. Use one to attach each 1-inch (2.5 cm) length of chain to the left outside loop on the ear hoop. In the following steps, use a jump ring to attach each sterling silve charm or drop to a chain link. Attach each bicone and pearl by opening the loop at the top of the head pin.

4. Attach one of the Celtic filigree charms to the left (outside) loop of the ear hoop.

5. From top to bottom along the chain, attach a bicone, pearl, small flat heart, bicone, and small puff heart in the last link (figure 1).

fig. 1

6. Attach a 1-inch (2.5 cm) length of chain to the right (outside) loop of the ear hoop. Also attach a decorative heart to the right loop of the ear hoop. Add the same bicones, charms, drops, and pearls—in the same order and positions—to this chain.

fig. 2

7. Attach the 1⅜-inch (3.5 cm) length of chain to the center loop of the ear hoop. Attach a pearl to this same loop. From top to bottom along this chain, attach a bicone, two small flat heart drops, two bicones, a pearl, and a large heart to the last link (figure 2).

8. Repeat the steps to make the second earring.

amber nights

Amber glass beads hand made by the designer are the focal point of these easy-to-make baubles.

Instructions

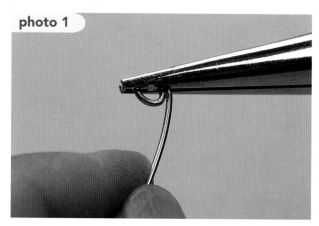

photo 1

1. Cut a piece of wire about 6 inches (15.5 cm) long to wire your focal bead. Make a spiral on one end (photo 1).

Designer: Kimberley Adams

Finished size: 2 inches (5.1 cm)

Materials

Approximately 20 inches (51 cm) of 20-gauge gold wire

2 focal beads

10 size 6 seed beads in color to complement focal bead

10 size 8 seed beads in color to complement focal bead and contrast with the other seed beads

Tools

Round-nose pliers

Chain-nose pliers

Spool (with or without thread)

photo 2

2. Add the focal bead, one size 6 seed bead, and one size 8 seed bead. Secure them with a loop on top (photo 2).

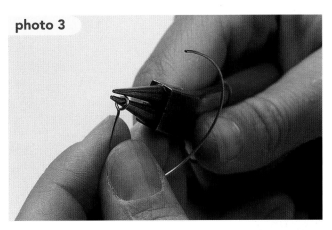

photo 3

3. Cut a 4-inch (10.5-cm) piece of wire for the hoop. Use the spool as a form to shape the piece into a circle. With round-nose pliers, make a loop at one end, then adjust the loop slightly to make sure it's centered over the rest of the wire (photo 3).

photo 4

4. From the other end, string on two size 8 beads, two size 6 beads, the focal bead, two size 6 beads, and two size 8 beads (photo 4).

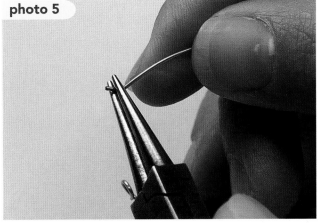

photo 5

5. Using chain-nose pliers, bend the other end of the wire at a right angle (photo 5). Hook the bent end into the loop to close the earring. Repeat the steps to make the second earring.

santa fe

This classic design incorporates painted wooden focal beads. Create a pair to match every color and style in your wardrobe.

photo 1

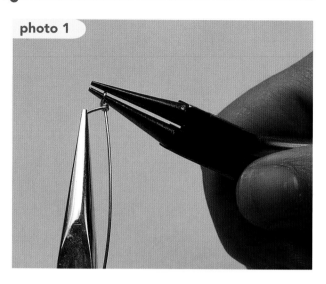

1. Cut a 6-inch (15-cm) piece of wire. Make a loop at one end (photo 1).

Designer: Linda Rose Nall

Finished size: 2½ inches (6.4 cm)

Materials

16–18 inches (41-46 cm) of 22-gauge sterling silver wire

4 amber chip beads

2 round amethyst beads, 5 mm

2 painted wooden focal beads

1 pair of silver ear wires

Tools

Round-nose pliers

Chain-nose pliers

Wire cutters

Jewelry hammer and anvil (optional)

2. String an amber chip bead, a focal bead, and a second amber chip bead (photo 2). Make a second wire loop at the top of the wire to hold the beads in place.

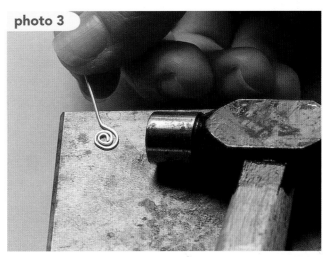

3. Cut a 2-inch (5-cm) piece of wire. Create a spiral at one end. To achieve a contemporary look, gently flatten the spiral using a jewelry hammer and anvil (photo 3).

4. Add an amethyst bead above the spiral, and use a wire loop at the top to attach this second piece to the base of the earring (photo 4).

5. Attach the earring to an ear wire (photo 5). Repeat the steps to make the second earring. Make sure the spiral on the second earring twists in the opposite direction from the spiral on the first.

extravagance

The combination of crystals and pearls will make you feel like royalty.

Designer: Melody MacDuffee	

Finished size: 1½ inches (3.8 cm) long and 1 inch (2.5 cm) wide

Materials

40 inches (101.6 cm) of 28-gauge craft wire or dead-soft sterling silver wire

10 white 3-mm pearls

6 crystal AB 3- to 4-mm bicones or fire-polished beads

28 white 2-mm pearls

26 silver-lined size 11° crystal seed beads

2 white 6-mm pearls (for center drop)

2 silver head pins

1 pair of silver ear wires

Tools

Wire cutters

Round-nose pliers

Chain-nose pliers

Metal file

Instructions

1. Cut a 1-foot (30.5 cm) piece of wire.

2. Make a Five-Petal Flower Motif, as follows. Add five 3-mm pearls (these are the "petals") to your wire and slide them to its center point. (**Note:** From this point on, the wires on either side of your beads will be referred to as two separate wires.) Form the beads into a loop, with the wires crossed at its base (figure 1). Secure the loop in place by wrapping one of the wires (this will be the working wire) around the other (now the dormant wire) twice, very tightly, right up against the base of the loop (figure 2).

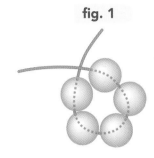

fig. 1

3. Bring your working wire all the way under the loop and then back over, across the front of it. Add a bicone or a fire-polished bead and position it in the center of your loop (figure 3).

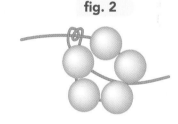

fig. 2

4. Holding the two wires between the thumb and forefinger of your left hand, right up against the base of your loop, give the loop two or three half-twists, just enough to secure it in place.

5. Back your left hand away from this twisted portion bit by bit, still holding your two wires just slightly apart, between the thumb and forefinger of your left hand, as you twist the motif with your right hand, thus beginning your main stem. Keep twisting until the main stem is ¼ to ⅜ inch (6 to 9.5 mm) long (figure 4). This motif is the bottom-center point of the earring.

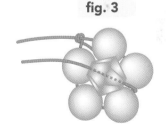

fig. 3

6. Using five 2-mm pearls for the petals and a seed bead for the center, and working on the left side of the main stem, make a Five-Petal Flower Motif on a branch ⅜ inch (9.5 mm) long. Twist a ¼- to ⅜-inch (6 to 9.5 mm) long section of main stem.

7. Repeat step 6 on the same side of the main stem.

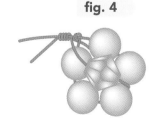

fig. 4

8. Add a seed bead, a 2-mm pearl, and a seed bead to your working wire and slide them down toward the main stem. Hold them ¼ inch (6 mm) from the main stem and form a loop, with the wires crossed at the loop's base.

9. Secure the loop in place by wrapping the loose end of your working wire around the part between the motif and your main stem twice, very tightly, right up against the base of the loop.

10. Back your left hand away from the twisted portion bit by bit, still holding your two wires just slightly apart between the thumb and forefinger of your left hand as you twist the motif with your right hand. Continue until the branch is twisted all the way back to the main stem. This is called a Three-Bead Single-Leaf Motif. Twist the main stem for ¼ to ⅜ inch (6 to 9.5 mm).

11. Repeat steps 8 through 10 on the same side of the main wire.

12. Attach a 10-inch (25.4 cm) piece of wire to the first Five-Petal Flower Motif you made. To do so, fold the wire (the one 10 inches [25.4 cm] long) in half, and place the fold across the twisted section at the base of the motif (photo 1, shown in greed beads). Bring the wires up behind the motif and thread them one at a time down through the motif from front to back, placing them one bead apart from each other. Pull them tight (photo 2, shown in green beads). Again, bring the wires up behind the motif and thread them one at a time down through the motif from front to back, placing them one bead apart from each other. You should be able to hold the piece by the new wires without it flopping down as if it were hinged. If it flops, thread the wires through the motif again, changing the locations of the wires a bit to make the "join" more stable. Next, flip the piece over and twist a ¼- to ⅜-inch (6 to 9.5 mm) section of main stem.

13. Repeat steps 6 through 10, making this side of the earrings as close as possible a mirror image of the first set. Set aside.

14. Make a second component by repeating all steps, making sure the lengths of the stems and branches of this component match the first one as closely as possible.

15. Using round-nose pliers, gently curve the branches of the motifs downward and open up a space in the center.

16. To each headpin, add a 6-mm pearl, a seed bead, and a bicone. Make wrapped loops at the top of each. This completes the center drops.

17. Bring the four wire tails of one of the components together, forming the loop of the earring, and then release one tail (this will be used in the next step to make the loop from which the center drop will dangle). Give the three other tails three half-twists.

18. Wrap the fourth tail once around the nearest section of main stem to secure it as closely as possible to the top of the earring. Thread it through the wrapped loop of one of the center drops. Leaving a ¼-inch (6 mm) length of wire, wrap the tail around the top portion of the other side of the earring at least twice until it's secure. If necessary, insert round-nose pliers into the loop to round it out.

19. Treating the three tails as one, add a bicone or a fire-polished bead, pushing it down close to the top of the earring, and then make a wrapped loop. Attach this loop to the ear wire.

20. Repeat steps 17 to 19 to finish the other earring.

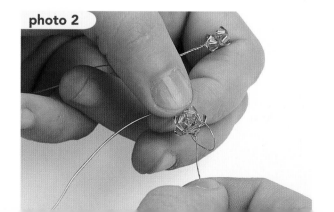

photo 1

photo 2

Cascading from a filigree disk, richly colored beads, crystals, and rhinestones dangle on chains of varying finishes.

Finished size: 4 inches (10.2 cm)

Materials

4 topaz-color prong-set rhinestones with loop, 5 mm

2 topaz-color rhinestone tri-beads (center-drilled), 12 mm

4 bronze-color glass rondelles, 4 mm

2 bronze-color fire polish glass beads, 4 mm

2 bronze fire polish glass beads, 3 mm

4 copper glass nailhead beads, 5 mm

2 light gold pearls (potato), 3 mm

2 amber-color crystals (round), 3 mm

Base metal rondelle (flat), 4 mm

2 amber crystals (round), 7 mm

2 jade cubes, 6 mm

2 bronze pearls (potato), 4 mm

2 filigree links, 7 mm

2 black diamond AB glass briolettes, 7 mm

2 metallized leaf charms, 28 mm

2 copper-color filigree disks, 15 mm

8 sterling silver head pins, 2 inches (5 cm) long

14 oval copper jump rings, 5 mm

2 straight-front leg niobium ear wires

6-inch (15.2 cm) length of 28-gauge copper-color wire

6-inch (15.2 cm) length of 28-gauge black wire

Instructions

1. If you're using new chain, age the metal by brushing it with the black metallic nail polish. Also tone down bright silver wires and the gold backing on the rhinestones with the nail polish.

2. Cut a 3-inch (7.6 cm) piece of copper wire. Make a wrapped loop at one end, at the same time adding a rhinestone in a setting with a loop. Thread a 4-mm glass rondelle and then a 4-mm fire polish glass bead. Finish with a wrapped loop, at the same time attaching the loop to the last link in a 2-inch (5 cm) piece of chain. On a head pin, thread a 3-mm fire polish and a nailhead bead. Make a wrapped loop at the top while attaching this dangle midway along the length of chain with the dangle at the bottom. On another head pin, thread a small, light gold potato pearl and an amber crystal, and then wrap the top while securing this dangle ⅜ inch (9.5 mm) from the top of the same chain.

3. Thread the flat rondelle onto a head pin. Insert the head pin through the filigree disk, from back to front, and add the rhinestone tri-bead. Make a wrapped loop on the front, at the same time attaching the top of the chain dangle that you made in step 2 (figure 1). To secure the tri-bead, weave the black wire through the filigree disk and around the rondelle on the back of the disk.

4. Thread a small amber crystal onto a head pin, and attach it to the last link of a 1½-inch (3.8 cm) piece of chain with a wrapped loop.

5. Thread a copper glass nail head bead, glass rondelle, jade cube, and bronze potato pearl onto a head pin. Finish with a wrapped loop, at the same time attaching it to a filigree link bead.

6. Using an oval jump ring, attach a metallized leaf to the last link of a 1-inch (2.5 cm) length of chain.

7. Insert a 3-inch (7.6 cm) length of sterling silver wire through a briolette and finish with a triangular wire wrap, at the same time attaching the drop to the last link of a 1¼-inch (3.2 cm) piece of crystal link chain.

fig. 1

side view

Materials (continued)

6-inch (15.2 cm) length of 28-gauge sterling silver wire

6 pieces of silver-color and gold-color 2.5 to 3 mm link chain; 2 lengths each of 1, 1½, and 2 inches (2.5, 3.8, and 5 cm)

2½-inch (6.4 cm) length of 3 mm crystal link chain

Black metallic nail polish

Tools

Chain-nose pliers, 2 pair

Round-nose pliers

Wire cutters

Ruler

Designer's Tips

All the chain in this project came from the designer's broken-treasures collection. Be on the lookout for vintage beads at thrift stores and garage sales. You can buy broken jewelry and then take the pieces apart for the components.

8. Add the chain dangles to the bottom of the disk, attaching each one with an oval jump ring, as shown in photo 1. Also attach the set rhinestone using an oval jump ring.

photo 1

9. Thread a large amber crystal on the front leg of the ear wire, and attach the embellished disk to the loop.

10. Repeat all steps to make a second earring, reversing the order of the chains so they mirror the first earring.

follies chandeliers

Beaded tendrils dangle from a larger bead that's framed by an unusual herringbone weave. The result is an airy design—daringly long, yet light as a feather.

Designer: Eni Oken

Finished size: 2⅜ inches (6.1 cm)

Materials

2 deep-red faceted flat pears,* ½ inch (1.3 cm) diameter

2 deep-red faceted rondelles, 9 mm diameter

4 deep-red flat pears,* ⅜ inch (9.5 mm) diameter

8 deep-red round beads, 5 mm diameter

2 deep-red faceted rondelles, 10 mm diameter

26-gauge sterling dead-soft silver wire, 6 feet (1.8 m) long

24-gauge sterling dead-soft silver wire, 8 inches (20.3 cm) long

2 sterling silver lever-back ear wires

Tools

Wire cutters

Ruler

Round-nose pliers

Flat-nose pliers

* Flat pears are sometimes called briolettes.

Instructions

1. Make the central dangles. Cut two pieces of 26-gauge wire 3 inches (7.6 cm) long. Slip a ½-inch (1.3 cm) flat pear on each of them and use a 1-inch (2.5 cm) tail to make wrapped bead loops, trimming any excess off the tails.

2. With the remaining wire and round-nose pliers, form small wrapped loops as close as possible to the ones you just made. Wind the wire on top of the previous wrapping; this gives the fine wire a more substantial appearance. Trim the wires closely.

3. Cut two pieces of 26-gauge wire 3 inches (7.6 cm) long. Make two wrapped loop bead links with a 9-mm rondelle on each, catching a ½-inch (1.3 cm) flat pear dangle at one end of each of the links. Trim off any extra wire.

4. Make the four side dangles, as you did in steps 1 and 2, using ½-inch (1.3 cm) flat pears instead.

5. Fabricate four smaller dangles from 4-inch (10.2 cm) lengths of 26-gauge wire. Make four wrapped bead loop links with two 5-mm beads each, catching a dangle from step 4 in one end of each. Trim away any extra wire.

6. Cut a piece of 24-gauge wire 4 inches (10.2 cm) long. Make a wrapped loop near one end, wrapping as many times as necessary to create a shank that's ¼ inch (0.6 cm) long. (Counting the number of times you wrap will help you replicate the shank on the opposite side of the bead.)

7. Slip a 10-mm rondelle onto the working end of the wire and make another ¼-inch (0.6 cm) shank with a wrapped loop on the other end of the wire, attaching the dangle you made in step 1 into the loop before you wrap it closed (see figure 1). Trim the ends of the wires with a flush cutter.

fig. 1

8. To craft a herringbone weave around the 10-mm rondelle, cut a piece of 26-gauge wire 2½ feet (76.2 cm) long. Secure the wire by wrapping it twice around one of the shanks, near the bead. Trim the tail. Bring the working wire down one side of the bead, and clockwise around the shank, from front to back, positioning the wire as close to the bead as possible; do the same on the other side of the bead. This completes one entire herringbone weave around the bead.

9. Repeat to complete five full weaves around the bead. As you progress, snug the wire against the bead's sides.

10. Weave the top of a sixth herringbone, but before wrapping the wire on the lower shank, slip one of the smaller-bead dangles onto the wire. Twist a small loop at the 4 o'clock position. After weaving the wire around the lower shank, make another small loop at the 8 o'clock position for another dangle. Bring the wire to the top shank, wrap it tightly twice around it, and trim any extra wire.

11. Repeat steps 6 through 10 for the other earring.

12. Attach the ear wires to the empty loops at the ends of the shanks.

enchantment

Designer: Patty Cox

Finished size: 2¹⁄₈ inches (5.4 cm)

Materials

2 amethyst bicone faceted beads, 6 mm

18 inches (45.7 cm) of 24-gauge gold wire

2 gold headpins, 1 inch (2.5 cm) long

2 French hook earring findings

Tools

Round-nose pliers

Nylon-jaw pliers

Wire cutters

Jig

Use a jig to create these enchanting dangles accented with a lovely figure-8 pattern and amethyst drops.

Instructions

1. Cut a 9-inch (22.9 cm) length of 24-gauge gold wire. Place pegs in jig according to figure 1.

2. Form a small loop in one wire end with round-nose pliers. Place loop on top peg of jig. Wrap wire around pegs according to diagram. Form wire loop at bottom peg. Remove wire from jig and cut wire tail.

3. Flatten wire with nylon-jaw pliers.

4. Thread an amethyst bicone bead on a headpin. Cut wire tail of headpin to ½ inch (1.3 cm).

5. Using round-nose pliers, form a loop in wire end. Attach loop to bottom loop of filigree piece.

6. Bend filigree top loop perpendicular to the flattened design.

7. Repeat steps 1-6 to make a second earring.

8. Attach the top filigree loop of each piece to an ear wire.

fig. 1

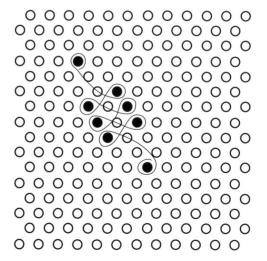

rain

Designer: Jan Loney

Finished size: 3 inches (7.6 cm long)

Materials

15 inches (38.1 cm) of 18-gauge silver wire

6 freshwater pewter pearls, 8 mm each

Stud and ball earring findings with eye

Tools

Hammer

Wire cutters

Flat-nose pliers

Instructions

1. Snip two pieces of wire, each 3½ inches (9 cm) long.

2. Cut two more pieces of wire, each 2½ inches (6.5 cm) long.

3. Cut two more pieces of wire, each 1½ inches (3.8 cm) long.

4. Slide a pearl onto each piece of wire.

5. Working with one piece of wire at a time, slide a pearl up the wire to the top. Use the cross peen hammer to flatten out each bottom end of the wire pieces into a slight fan shape. This will keep the pearl from sliding off the end of the wire. Slide the pearl back down until it stops.

6. Form an eye on the end of each piece of wire. Attach three of the pearl/wire pieces, each of a different length, to the loop of each earring stud. Using pliers, close wire eyes around the loop of stud.

Silver wire and pearls make lovely earrings, flowing with ease and elegance.

pearl bouquet

Delicate pearl bouquets are wonderful adornments for any lobe. Create these earrings by linking beaded dangles to a short chain.

Designer: Lisa M. Call

Finished size: 1 inch (2.5 cm)

Materials

2 white freshwater pearls, 5 x 7-mm top-drilled teardrop

2 white freshwater pearls, 5-mm keishi

2 white freshwater pearls, 5-mm round

2 mauve freshwater pearls, 5-mm button

2 peach freshwater pearls, 5-mm button

2 mauve freshwater pearls, 4-mm round

2 white freshwater pearls, 4-mm button

2 peach freshwater pearls, 3-mm round

2 white topaz or quartz faceted rondelles, 3 mm

14 sterling silver 24-gauge head pins, 1½ inches (3.8 cm) long

2 sterling silver 24-gauge ball-end head pins, 1½ inches (3.8 cm) long

2 sterling silver lever back or French hook earring findings

2-inch (5.1 cm) length of 2.5-mm oval link sterling silver chain

9-inch (22.9 cm) length of 26-gauge sterling silver wire

Tools

Chain-nose pliers

Round-nose pliers

Wire cutters

Instructions

1. Cut the chain into two 1-inch (2.5 cm) pieces. Set aside.

2. Cut two 4½-inch (11.4 cm) pieces of wire. Set aside.

3. String one top-drilled pearl onto a piece of wire. Let the pearl slide one-third of the way down the wire. Cross the wire ends at the top of the pearl to form a triangle.

fig. 1

4. Use chain-nose pliers to grasp the short wire where the two wires cross. Bend the short wire so it points straight up from the top of the pearl. Bend the long wire so it sits at a 90° angle from the short wire (figure 1).

5. Tightly wrap the long wire around the short wire one time. Continue to coil the wire down toward the pearl to make a cone shape (figure 2). Trim the long wire and use chain-nose pliers to tighten the wrap.

fig. 2

6. Make a wrapped loop with the short wire that attaches to the end link of one of the chains. Continue making the wrap until it meets the beginning of the coil you made in the previous step (figure 3). Attach the other end of the chain to an ear wire.

fig. 3

7. Slide a 5-mm white pearl onto a regular head pin. Make a wrapped loop that attaches to the fifth link on the chain (the same link that holds the teardrop pearl dangle). Slip a 5-mm peach pearl onto a regular head pin. Make a wrapped loop that attaches to the same chain link, this time on the other side of the teardrop dangle. Continue adding two pearl dangles to each chain link, adding one 5-mm mauve pearl dangle and one keishi pearl dangle on the fourth link. (*Note:* Use a ball-end head pin to make the keishi dangle so it resembles a flower.) Add one 4-mm white pearl dangle and one 4-mm mauve pearl dangle to the third link; add one 3-mm peach pearl dangle and one white topaz dangle to the second link.

8. Repeat steps 3 through 7 to make the second earring.

louise

Flirty and a bit bohemian, these earrings take advantage of the visual weight of filigree. While they look almost too heavy to wear, they're actually light as feathers.

Designer: Cynthia Deis

Finished size: 3 inches (7.5 cm)

Materials

2 antiqued brass six-point dapped filigree flowers, 20 mm

2 antiqued brass six-point flat filigree flowers, 20 mm

2 antiqued brass filigree rings, 32 mm

2 peach crystal round beads, 6 mm

2 amber flat diamond glass beads with gold-colored design, 7 x 12 mm

2 antiqued brass head pins, 2 inches (5.1 cm)

6 antiqued brass oval jump rings, 4 x 5 mm

1 pair of antiqued brass ear wires

Medium-width flexible beading wire, 12 inches (30.5 cm)

Tools

Chain-nose pliers

Round-nose pliers

Wire cutters

Instructions

1. Pass a head pin through the edge of a filigree ring from inside to outside (figure 1). Slip on one round bead and form a wrapped loop to secure the bead. Set aside.

2. Cut a 6-inch (15.2 cm) length of wire and string on a diamond bead, leaving a 3-inch (7.6 cm) tail. Sew the bead to the center of one of the dapped flowers. Tie a square knot on the back of the flower to firmly seat the bead. Trim the wire ends.

3. Place the dapped flower on top of one of the flat flowers so their backs touch. Use a jump ring to connect each of the petal sets.

4. Attach one of the jump rings on the flower to the wrapped loop formed in step 1 (figure 2). This is the bottom of the earring.

5. Use a jump ring to attach the ear wire to the jump ring at the top of the earring.

6. Repeat the steps to make the second earring.

fig. 1

fig. 2

divine

Showcase exquisite padparadschas (the rarest naturally occurring colored crystal) and beautiful polygon crystals in these sweet earrings.

Designer: Bonnie Clewans

Finished sizes: Angel earrings, 1¾ inches (4.4 cm);
Crystal Bow earrings 1⅝ inches (4.1 cm)

Angel Materials

2 crystals (polygon), 12 mm

2 pearls (round), 6 mm

2 rhinestone rondelles, 5 mm

2 bicone crystals, 3 mm

2 gold plated pewter angel wings, 8 mm

2 gold filled head pins, 2 inches (5 cm) long

2 lever back ear wires

Crystal Bow Materials

2 padparadscha crystals (cube), 8 mm

2 faceted crystals (round), 3 mm

2 silver plated pewter bows, 10 mm

2 sterling silver head pins, 2 inches
(5 cm) long

2 lever back, gold filled ear wires

8-inch (20.3 cm) length of 24-gauge
half-hard sterling silver wire

Tools

Round-nose pliers

Fine wire cutters

Crimp tool

Ruler

Glue

Instructions

fig. 1

1. To make an Angel earring, thread a polygon crystal, angel wings, a pearl, a rondelle, and a bicone onto a head pin (figure 1).

2. Finish the dangle with a wrapped head pin. Use the crimp tool to tuck in any excess wire, taking care not to crush the top bead.

3. Carefully open the loop on the ear wire, slip on the dangle, and close the ear wire loop.

4. Repeat steps 1 through 3 to make a second earring.

fig. 2

5. To make a Crystal Bow earring, thread a cube onto a head pin. Cut the wire into two 4-inch (10.2 cm) lengths. Set on piece of wire aside to make the matching ea ring later. Position the round-nose pliers 1½ inches (3.8 cm) from the top of the remaining piece of wire. Holding the wire below the pliers, bend the wire away from you to make a right angle. Pull the wire over the top of the round-nose of the pliers. Remove the pliers. Thread the wire-wrapped cube onto the loop. Holding the open loop tightly with the round-nose pliers, wrap the short end of the wire around the long end three times. Trim off the excess wire on the short end only. Thread the bow and round crystal onto the wire (figure 2). Make a wrapped loop above the crystal.

6. Repeat step 5 to make a matching Crystal Bow earring.

Designer's Tip

You can paint the angel wings with nail polish or enamel model paint if you want to add more color.

spellbound

These earrings offer color and movement with their cascading tiers of beautiful garnet beads.

Designer: Valérie MacCarthy

Finished size: 3½ inches (8.9 cm)

Materials

16 garnet beads, 7 mm

6 garnet beads, 4 mm

8-inch (20.3 cm) length of 1-mm gold-filled chain

18-inch (45.7 cm) length of 22-gauge gold-filled wire

32-inch (81.2 cm) length of 26-gauge gold-filled wire

Tools

Round-nose pliers

Chain-nose pliers

Wire cutters

Large rubberized round-nose pliers

Ruler

Instructions

1. With wire cutters, cut off a 5-inch (12.7 cm) segment of the 22-gauge wire. Set aside this segment, as it will be used later to make the ear wires.

2. Cut the remaining 13 inches (33 cm) of 22-gauge wire in half, making two 6½-inch (16.5 cm) segments. These two pieces will be used to build the hangers from which all the stones dangle. (You could use a jig for making the wire base, but I prefer using round-nose pliers.)

3. Select one of the 6½-inch (16.5 cm) segments. Use the round-nose pliers to grip the middle of it. Wrap the wire one full turn to make a loop.

4. Hold this loop with the chain-nose pliers. Twist the wires around to secure.

5. Using the round-nose pliers again, place only the tip of one jaw in the center of the loop. Lightly grip the twist you just made and wrap the wires downward to make a second smaller loop. After the two wires have crossed, remove the round-nose pliers, hold onto this smaller loop with the chain-nose pliers, and twist again. The wires should now be horizontal with the loops on top (figure 1).

fig. 1

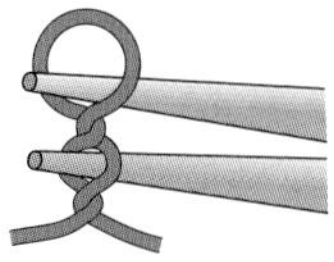

6. Place the round-nose pliers on one side of the loop in the wire, approximately ¼ inch (6 mm) away. Loop the wire around the jaw of the pliers.

7. Repeat this same action again ¼ inch (6 mm) away, this time wrapping the wire around a bit further down on the jaw of the pliers to make a larger loop. Continue wrapping the wire until you've wrapped around one and one-half times.

fig. 2

8. Repeat steps 6 and 7 on the other side of the loop (figure 2).

9. Using the rubberized round-nose pliers, slightly bend down the wire ends to give the hanger a pleasing curve. First, place the jaws of the pliers between the center loop and the smaller loop. Then nudge the end of the wire to shape it.

10. Repeat this between the smaller loop and the larger outer loop, nudging both sides to curve the hanger.

11. Repeat steps 9 and 10 on the other side to make both sides curve down slightly.

12. Now make the shortest dangle. Using the 26-gauge wire and the round-nose pliers, place the very end of the wire in the jaw tip of the pliers. Wrap the wire around the jaw two times. After making the first loop, open up the jaws, turn the loop, clamp down again, and complete the second circle. While the pliers are still in place, bend the wire 45° to center the circled wire (figure 3).

fig. 3

a   b

13. Slide a 4-mm bead onto the wire and bend the wire 45°. Wrap it around using the round-nose pliers and slide it onto the end of the chain. Use the chain-nose pliers to hold onto this loop. Wrap the wire around to secure. For this design, wrap the wire around the tops of the beads numerous times. If you would like to create this effect, continue wrapping the wire around and around until you are pleased with the look of it. Cut off the excess wire. You may also want to use the chain-nose pliers to gently press the tip of this wire inward, flush to the other wraps. This will prevent it from catching and possibly unraveling.

14. With the wire cutters, cut the attached chain ¼ inch (6 mm) from the bead.

15. Using the round-nose pliers, make a new loop with the 26-gauge wire. Slide the end of the chain onto the loop and wrap the loop closed. Slide on another 4-mm bead. Bend the wire 45° and make a new loop, this time a bit further along on the wire than usual. Slide the wire through the lower center loop on the wire hanger and pull it through.

16. Using the very tips of the chain-nose pliers, hold this loop beneath the wire hanger and wrap the wire around again to secure.

17. Now make the medium dangle. Start by making the end of this dangle. Repeat steps 12 and 13, this time using a 7-mm bead. Slide two ½-inch (1.3 cm) lengths of chain onto the top loop of the bead.

18. Attach a wire loop link with a 7-mm bead at the end of one piece of chain. Bend the wire and place it through one of the smaller loops on either side of the wire hanger. Wrap it closed to secure. Repeat with the remaining piece of chain, attaching it to the other smaller loop on the opposite side of the wire hanger.

19. Finally, make the longest dangle. Again starting from the end and working out, repeat steps 12 and 13, but use two beads, one 4-mm bead followed by one 7-mm bead. Attach two ¼-inch (6 mm) lengths of chain to this piece.

20. Make a wire loop link through one piece of chain and add another 7-mm bead. Before you close the loop, add a ⅜-inch (9.5 mm) segment of chain. Add a new wire loop link and 7-mm bead to the end of this piece of chain. Attach one last ¼-inch (6 mm) length of chain before you wrap the loop closed. Repeat this step on the remaining piece of chain you added in step 19.

21. Make a new loop in the 26-gauge wire and place one chain end onto the loop. Hold the loop with the chain-nose pliers and twist the wire around to secure. Cut off the shorter wire. Now loop the wire again and pass it through one of the end loops on the hanger. Hold the loop and wrap the wire around the twist. Cut off the excess.

22. Repeat step 21 with the remaining piece of chain.

23. Now make the ear wire. Take the 5-inch (12.7 cm) length of 22-gauge wire that you set aside in step 1. Cut it into two 2½-inch (6.4 cm) segments. Hold one of the wires with the round-nose pliers about ½ inch (1.3 cm) from the end. Loop the wire around. Slide the loop through the top loop of the hanger. Hold the loop with the chain-nose pliers and twist the wires around to secure. Cut off the shorter wire.

24. Hold the wire with the rubberized round-nose pliers and loop the wire around to form the actual ear wire. Cut the wire to the desired length.

25. Now grip the very end of this same wire with the chain-nose pliers and bend it slightly upward to add a finishing detail.

26. Repeat steps 3 through 25 to make the second earring.

twinkling leaf

This lovely earring design combines natural brass filigree with green garnet, clear quartz, and green crystal. The brass and beads chime as you wear these earrings, evoking an enchanted glade with a hint of sparkle—is that a garden sprite peeking out of its golden cage?

Designer: Cynthia Deis

Finished size: 1½ inches (3.8 cm)

Materials

2 natural brass four-petal filigree bead caps, 12 mm

4 natural brass filigree bead caps, 8 mm

8 natural brass filigree leaves, 5 x 7 mm

2 green garnet rondelle beads, 10 mm

2 crystal quartz rondelle beads, 8 mm

2 tourmaline green crystal round beads, 4 mm

2 copper head pins, 2 inches (5.1 cm)

8 natural brass round jump rings, 5 mm

2 natural brass oval decorative jump rings (from chain), 5 x 10 mm

1 pair of copper ear wires

Tools

Round-nose pliers

Wire cutters

Chain-nose pliers

Instructions

1. Slip one petal bead cap, outside to inside, onto a head pin. Add one 10-mm bead and use your fingers to gently press the bead into the cap so the curves match. Slide on one bead cap from inside to outside and form a simple loop to secure the caps and bead (figure 1). Keep the trimmed end handy. Set the dangle aside.

2. Use a round jump ring to connect one leaf to the hole on one of the points of a filigree bead cap (figure 2). Make sure that the leaf faces outward. Repeat on each point of the cap.

3. Form a simple loop at the end of the leftover wire from step 1. Slip on one 8-mm bead, one 4-mm bead, and a four-petal bead cap from inside to outside. The beads should nestle within the cap. Form a simple loop to secure the beads and cap. Set the beaded link aside.

4. Use chain-nose pliers to gently open an oval jump ring. Slide on the dangle and beaded link and close the ring.

5. Add an ear wire to the open loop at the top of the earring.

6. Repeat the steps to make the second earring.

fig. 1

fig. 2

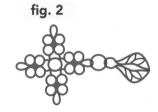

masquerade

Designer: Melody MacDuffee

Finished size: 1½ inches (3.8 cm) long, not including ear wires

Materials

7 inches (17.8 cm) of 20-gauge gold half-hard wire

10 feet (3 m) of 28-gauge craft wire or dead-soft gold-filled wire

Size 13° or 15° seed beads, preferably charlotte-cut:
- 82 copper
- 72 silver
- 64 gold

68 white 3- to 4-mm freshwater pearls

1 pair of gold ear wires

66 head pins

Tools

Wire cutters

Round-nose pliers

Chain-nose pliers

Metal file

With undeniable grace and an air of mystery, these are the perfect accessories for a night on the town.

FIVE-PETAL FLOWER MOTIF

1. Add five copper charlottes to your wire and slide them down to its center point. These are the petals. (**Note**: From this point on, the wires on either side of your beads will be referred to as two separate wires.) Form the beads into a loop with the wires crossed at its base. Secure the loop in place by wrapping one of your wires (this will be your working wire) around the other (now your dormant wire) twice very tightly right up against the base of the loop.

2. Bring your working wire all the way under the loop and then back over across the front of it. Add a silver charlotte and position it in the center of your loop (figure 2).

fig. 2

3. Holding your two wires between the thumb and forefinger of your left hand right up against the base of your loop, give the loop two or three half-twists, just enough to secure it in place.

4. Back your left hand away from the twisted portion bit by bit, still holding the two wires just slightly apart between the thumb and forefinger of your left hand as you twist the motif with your right, thus beginning your main stem. Keep twisting until the main stem is ¼ inch (6 mm) long.

● Instructions

1. Cut the 20-gauge wire in half. Curve each wire to make a bottom-heavy oval shape that is slightly open at the top. Using round-nose pliers, curl a closed loop toward the back side of the frame at each end of each oval (figure 1).

2. Cut the 28-gauge wire into two 2-foot (61 cm) pieces and two 3-foot (0.9 m) pieces.

3. Using one of the 2-foot (61 cm) pieces, and using copper charlottes for the petals and a silver one for the center, make a Five-Petal Flower Motif at the center point of the wire (see box at left).

4. Using silver charlottes, make a Three-Bead Single-Leaf Motif (see box on page 123). Add a gold charlotte to each wire, and twist a ⅜-inch (9.5 mm) section of main stem.

5. On each side of the main stem, make a main branch with two sub-branches. Using *gold charlottes* for the petals and *copper ones* for the center, make a Five-Petal Flower Motif on a ¾-inch (1.9 cm) branch, twisting only one-third of the way back toward the main stem. This is the main branch. Using silver charlottes, make a Three-Bead Single-Leaf Motif on a ⅜-inch (9.5 mm) sub-branch off the main branch (see figure 3 on next page). Twist back to the main branch. Twist a ¼-inch (6 mm) section of main branch back toward the main stem. Using copper charlottes, make another Three-Bead Single-Leaf Motif on a ⅜-inch (9.5 mm) sub-branch off the main branch (see figure 4 on next page). Twist back to the main branch. Twist the main branch the rest of the way back to the main stem. Add a silver charlotte to each wire, and twist a ⅜-inch (9.5 mm) section of main stem (see figure 5 on next page).

fig. 1

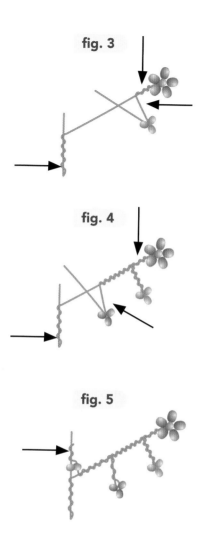

fig. 3

fig. 4

fig. 5

6. Using silver charlottes for the petals and gold ones for the centers, make a Five-Petal Flower Motif on a ¼-inch (6 mm) branch on each side of the main stem. Twist a ¼-inch (6 mm) section of the main stem.

7. Using copper charlottes for the petals and gold ones for the centers, make a Five-Petal Flower Motif on a ⅜-inch (9.5 mm) branch on each side of the main stem. Add a copper charlotte to each wire, and twist a ¼-inch (6 mm) section of the main stem.

8. Using gold charlottes, make a Three-Bead Single-Leaf Motif on a ¼-inch (6 mm) branch on each side of the main stem. Fasten off.

9. Repeat steps 3 through 8 for the other earring.

10. Using round-nose pliers, tweak the filigrees by gently curving the stems and branches as shown in the photograph, shaping them as needed so that they fit into the frames.

11. Using short scraps of 28-gauge wire, "tack" the filigrees temporarily in place on the frame at each projected point of contact (see figure 6). **Note:** The points of contact may differ slightly from those in the diagram. What is important is that the filigree lay comfortably and attractively inside the frame.

12. Using one of the 3-foot (0.9 m) pieces of 28-gauge wire, attach it to the top of one frame just below the closed loop by wrapping it two or three times in the appropriate spot. This is now the working wire. Coil tightly around the frame until you reach the first point of contact.

13. Remove the first "tacking" wire and coil the working wire once into the first motif. Continue coiling until you reach the next point of contact.

14. Repeat step 13 until all the points of contact have been anchored to the frame. Then continue coiling up to the frame's closed loop. Clip tails.

15. Repeat steps 10 through 14 for the other earring.

16. Using a leftover scrap of 28-gauge wire, add a gold charlotte, a pearl, and another gold charlotte. Center them on the wire and bring the ends of the wire up through the loops of one of the frames, from the inside to the outside of the oval. Bring each wire around and through the frame loop again, pulling them tightly to close up the top of the frame. Add two copper charlottes to each wire. Using the two wires as one, wire-wrap a loop. Clip the tails. Repeat the process for the other earring.

17. Attach an ear wire to each loop, making sure that the flowers are facing forward.

18. Add a gold charlotte and a pearl to each of the 20 head pins.

19. Wire-wrap one of the pins onto the bottom part of the hoop-loop (the coiled frame) as close as possible to the center point (on one side of the bottom copper flower).

20. Wire-wrap another pin to the loop of the previous wire wrap, placing it at the back side of the hoop-loop. Wire-wrap two more pins to that second wire-wrapped loop (again at the rear side of the hoop-loop, placing one on either side of the pearl), and then another to each of those loops. This completes the first center drop.

21. Repeat step 20 on the other side of the bottom copper flower. The second center drop is now made.

22. Repeat step 20 up through "placing one on either side of the pearl" on either side of the center drops.

23. Add a silver charlotte and a pearl to each of the 12 head pins. Working outward from one side of the cluster of gold-tipped drops, repeat step 20 up through "placing it at the back side of the hoop-loop" three times. Repeat for the other side of the earring.

24. Add a copper charlotte and a pearl to each of the remaining head pins. Working outward from one side of the cluster of silver-tipped drops, repeat step 20 up through "placing it at the back side of the hoop-loop" twice. Repeat for the other side of the earring.

25. Continuing to work outward from the center, wire-wrap single head pins holding copper charlottes and single pearls until the bottom section looks full. Use any leftover head pins to fill in gaps in the fringe.

THREE-BEAD SINGLE-LEAF MOTIF

1. Thread three silver charlottes on the wire and slide them toward the main stem. Holding them ⅜ inch (9.5 mm) from the main stem, form them into a loop with the wires crossed at the loop's base.

Shown in an alternate colorway.

2. Secure the loop in place by wrapping the loose end of your working wire twice around the part between this motif and the main stem, wrapping it very tightly and right up against the base of the loop.

3. Back your left hand away from the twisted portion bit by bit, still holding your two wires just slightly apart between the thumb and forefinger of your left hand as you twist the motif with your right hand. Continue until the branch is twisted all the way back to the main stem.

fig. 6

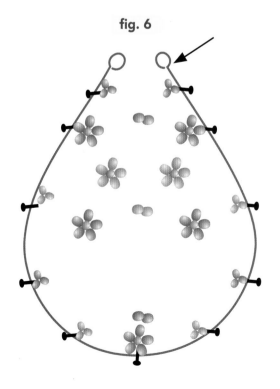

tuxedo

Perfect for a fancy event, these simple and elegant earrings use plain wire to highlight the beauty of the pearls. Let your pearls swing!

Designer: Jean Power

Finished size: 1¾ inches (4.4 cm)

Materials

2 lavender iris freshwater pearls, 10-mm potato

6-inch (15.2 cm) length of 20-gauge sterling silver wire

2 sterling silver earring findings

Tools

Bead reamer, optional

Ruler or measuring tape

Wire cutters

Bead tube or ½-inch (1.3 cm) dowel, 4 inches (10.2 cm) long

Round-nose pliers

Chain- or flat-nose pliers

Instructions

Note: You may need to use a bead reamer to enlarge the holes in your pearls if they don't fit on the 20-gauge wire. If you don't have a bead reamer, make the earrings with the thickest wire you can get through your pearls.

1. Cut the wire in two 3-inch (7.6 cm) pieces. Set aside.

2. Slide a pearl onto one of the wires and center it.

3. Holding the pearl in place, bend both wire ends around the tube until they cross (figure 1). Check that the pearl still sits in the center of the wire and that the wire ends are even.

4. Use chain-nose pliers to form a slight bend on each wire where the wires cross, or about ⅜ inch (9 mm) from each wire end (figure 2).

5. Form a simple loop at each wire end. Make sure the loops are the same size (figure 3). Use chain-nose pliers to squeeze the loops together so they sit next to each other. Set aside.

6. Use chain-nose pliers to grasp one of the ear wire's loops, right underneath the spot where the wire touches itself. Gently turn the loop 90°.

7. Attach the earring finding so it holds both simple loops.

8. Repeat steps 2 through 7 to make the second earring.

fig. 1

fig. 2

fig. 3

quatrefoil

Designer: Eni Oken

Finished size: 1½ inches (3.8 cm)

Materials

4 sea-green faceted briolettes, ⅜ inch (1 cm) long*

2 sea-green faceted briolettes, ½ inch (1.3 cm) long*

8 round faceted green crystal beads, 5 mm diameter

8 pearls, 2 mm diameter

2 lavender rose-montées (mounted rhinestones), 5 mm diameter

26-gauge dead-soft sterling silver wire, 4 feet (1.2 m) long

2 sterling silver lever-back ear wires

Tools

Wire cutters

Ruler

Flush cutter

Round-nose pliers

Flat-nose pliers

* Briolettes are also called flat pears.

Pearl, crystal, and rhinestone beads are transformed into a four-petaled focal point in these earrings. Sea-green briolette dangles complete the delicate design.

Instructions

1. Form the dangle chains: cut three 3-inch (7.6 cm) lengths of wire. Slip one end of a wire on a ½-inch (1.3 cm) briolette, leaving a 1-inch (2.5 cm) tail. Bring both wires together and wrap the shorter end around the longer one. Trim the short end with a flush cutter.

2. Form a small loop with the round-nose pliers on the longer end of the wire, as close as possible to the previous wrap. Wrap the wire on top of the previous wrap. Trim the wire very closely with the cutter.

3. Repeat steps 1 and 2, using two of the ⅜-inch (1 cm) briolettes.

4. Form a quatrefoil: cut a 9-inch (22.9 cm) length of wire. Slip four faceted round beads onto the wire and form a circle, twisting the wires together, with a 2-inch (5 cm) tail on one side.

fig. 1

5. Bring the longer end of the wire between the first and second bead and wrap it once around that part of the wire that is holding the four beads in their circle shape; the first bead is now framed by wire.

6. Use round-nose pliers to wrap the short end of the wire into a wrapped loop, which is at the 12 o'clock position.

7. Repeat step 5 between the second and third beads. Create a wrapped loop to hold a ½-inch (1.3 cm) briolette dangle here. Figure 1 shows what your work should look like.

8. Repeat step 5 for the third and fourth beads. The wire has gone all the way around the circle of beads and is now back at the top loop.

9. Pass the wire behind the loop and slip on a small pearl, a rose-montée, and another pearl. Bring the wire across the quatrefoil (to the 6 o'clock position) and wrap it firmly around the shank of the loop that holds the dangle. Trim the wire closely.

10. Cut a 6-inch (15.2 cm) length of wire. Slip it onto the rose-montée and add a pearl to each side. Attach it to the quatrefoil by wrapping it once onto the right side, between the first and second beads, and once on the left side, between the third and fourth beads.

11. Using round-nose pliers, wrap a loop on each side, slipping a dangle made in step 3 into each loop. Trim the excess wire.

12. Using flat-nose pliers, open the loop on the ear wire. Slip the earring on it and close the loop.

13. Repeat the steps to make the second earring.

far east

The ancient Chinese text of the *I Ching* describes a system for uncovering the order in chance events. In beading this project, you can follow the photo closely, or just see where chance takes you.

Designer: Terry Taylor

Finished size: 2¼ inches (5.7 cm) long

Materials

2 replica Chinese *I Ching* coins

4 brass or gold-filled head pins

4 small brass beads

8 small brass washer beads

8 African bronze beads

Dyed coral slices

2 bronze ear wires

Tools

Sharp nail or automatic center punch

Drill and small drill bit
(#60 or smaller)

Chain-nose pliers

Round-nose pliers

Wire cutters

Designer's Tip

Make the hanging lengths of beads as long as you wish. If you want to hang a third length on a coin, you'll need to choose smaller beads.

Instructions

1. Use the nail or center punch to make two evenly spaced marks along the lower edge of each coin. Make one mark directly opposite them, also along the coin's edge. Drill the three holes in each coin.

2. Thread the brass beads, brass washers, bronze beads, and coral slices onto the head pins. Thread the beads symmetrically, if you wish, or create subtle visual interest by varying the position of the small brass beads and washer beads.

3. Use the chain-nose and round-nose pliers to bend the straight end of a beaded head pin into the beginning loop for a wrapped loop. Thread the head pin onto a coin, and finish the wrapped loop. Trim any excess wire with wire cutters.

4. Repeat step 3 for each of the other three head pins.

5. Use chain-nose pliers to open one ear wire, attach the coin to the top hole, and then close. Repeat for the second coin.

diamonds

More is more
with these
shimmering
dangles.

Designer: Melody MacDuffee

Finished size: 1½ inches (3.8 cm) long
(not including ear wires) and 1¼ inches
(3.1 cm) at widest point

Materials

5 feet (1.5 m) of 28-gauge gold-filled
craft wire or dead-soft wire

4 mm bicone crystals:
   16 crystal AB
   6 beige

7 inches (17.8 cm) of 20-gauge
half-hard gold-filled wire

10 grams of AB size 15° crystal
seed beads

1 pair of gold ear wires

Tools

Wire cutters

Round-nose pliers

Chain-nose pliers

Metal file or emery board, optional

Instructions

1. Cut an 8-inch (20.3 cm) piece of 28-gauge wire. Using crystal AB for the petals and beige for the center, make a Five-Petal Flower Motif with Beaded Outline (see box at right).

2. Twist a ½-inch (1.3 cm) section of main stem.

3. Using beige, make a One-Bead Single-Leaf Motif with Beaded Outline (see box on next page) on a ½-inch (1.3 cm) branch on each side of the main stem (do not twist a section of main stem in between them). Finish off.

4. Repeat steps 1 through 3 for the other earring, making it as close to a mirror image of the first side as possible.

5. Cut the 20-gauge wire in half. Make a frame by bending one piece to a 90º angle at its center point, and then again along each side 1½ inches (3.8 cm) from the center bend. Make closed loops that face toward the center opening at each end. This completes the frame. Repeat for the other earring.

6. Using round-nose pliers, tweak the filigrees by gently curving the two leaf branches downward, shaping them as needed so that they fit into the frame.

Designer's Tip

If the frame is larger than needed, clip a small portion at a time from the closed loops, and re-curl them until the frames are the optimal size for the filigree, uncoiling one or more single-seed bead loops if necessary.

FIVE-PETAL FLOWER MOTIF WITH BEADED OUTLINE

1. Add five crystal ABs (these are the petals) to your wire and slide them down to its center point. (**Note**: From this point on, the wires on either side of your beads will be referred to as two separate wires.) Form the beads into a loop, with the wires crossed at its base. Secure the loop in place by wrapping one of the wires (this will be the working wire) around the other (now the dormant wire) twice, very tightly, right up against the base of the loop.

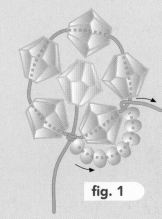

fig. 1

2. Bring the working wire all the way under the loop and then back over, across the front of it. Add a beige AB and position it in the center of the loop.

3. Holding the two wires between the thumb and forefinger of your left hand, right up against the base of the loop, give the loop two or three half-twists, just enough to secure it in place.

4. Add eight seed beads to the working wire and bring the wire up, from back to front, between the next two petals of the motif, pulling the wire tightly so that it forms an outline around the first bead, as shown in figure 1. Outline all the other petals in the same manner.

5. Holding your two wires between the thumb and forefinger of your left hand, right up against the base of your loop, give the loop two or three half-twists, just enough to secure it in place.

6. Back your left hand away from this twisted portion bit by bit, still holding your two wires just slightly apart between the thumb and forefinger of your left hand as you twist the motif with your right hand, thus beginning your main stem.

ONE-BEAD SINGLE-LEAF MOTIF WITH BEADED OUTLINE

1. Hold the bead at the called-for distance from the main stem (in this case, ½ inch [1.3 cm]), fold the wire back over the bead and, holding the two wires between the thumb and forefinger of your left hand right up against the base of your bead, give the loop two or three half-twists, just enough to secure it.

fig. 2

2. Add 16 seed beads to the working wire and loop them around the bicone, wrapping the tail twice around the base of the motif to secure the loop in place (figure 2).

3. Back your left hand away from the twisted portion bit by bit, still holding your two wires just slightly apart between the thumb and forefinger of your left hand as you twist the motif with your right hand. Continue until the branch is twisted all the way back to the main stem.

7. Using short scraps of 28-gauge wire, "tack" the filigree in place at each projected point of contact on the frames (i.e., the outer side of each leaf motif and the center points of the second and fourth petals of the flower).

8. Cut a 1½-foot (45.7 cm) length of 28-gauge wire, and attach it to the frame next to one of the closed loops by wrapping it two or three times around the frame.

9. Thread 19 seed beads onto the 28-gauge wire. Wrap the wire three times around the frame, then, as you wrap once more, stop to seat a seed bead on the outer edge of the frame. Hold the bead in place by pressing it against the frame with a finger, then wrap the wire three times around the frame. Continue around the frame in this manner, attaching all the seed beads to it. Anytime you reach a filigree tacked to the frame, catch it in the working wire so that you're both embellishing the frame with seed beads *and* permanently attaching the filigree to the frame. After you reach the opposite side of the frame, wrap the working wire three times. Cut off any excess wire and finish off.

10. Repeat steps 6 through 10 for the other earring.

11. Cut the remaining 28-gauge wire into six pieces.

12. Wire-wrap a loop at one end of one piece, add a crystal AB, and wire-wrap another loop. Attach one of these loops to one of the top loops of the frame. Repeat for the other side of the frame.

13. Repeat step 12 for the other earring.

14. Using one of the remaining pieces of 28-gauge wire, add a crystal AB. Thread the tails of wire through the top wire-wrapped loops of an earring. Add two seed beads to each tail. Bring the tails together and, treating the two wires as one, wire-wrap a loop. Attach this loop to the ear wire. Repeat for the other earring.

weeping willow

Add a natural touch to your wardrobe with these earthy earrings, accented with a touch of extra looping detail.

Designer: Valérie MacCarthy

Finished size: 2¾ inches (7 cm)

Materials

2 copper-colored pearls (disks), 10 mm

18 peridot beads, 4 mm

4 copper-colored pearls, 3 mm

6 green grossular garnet briolettes, 6 mm

4 gold-filled beads, 3 mm

6 gold-filled ball-end head pins, 1 inch (2.5 cm) long

2 gold-filled ball-end head pins, 1½ inches (3.8 cm) long

8-inch (20.3 cm) length of 1.5-mm gold-filled chain

24-inch (61 cm) length of 26-gauge gold-filled wire

Tools

Chain-nose pliers

Round-nose pliers

Wire cutters

Large rubberized round-nose pliers

Ruler

Instructions

1. Make the ear wires using the 1½-inch (3.8 cm) ball-end head pins. Place the round-nose pliers around the end with the ball. Loop the head pin around until the ball is touching the wire. Use the rubberized round-nose pliers to grip the wire above the loop just created. Bend the wire around the pliers (figure 1). Using the chain-nose pliers, slightly bend up the tip of the wire end for a finishing touch.

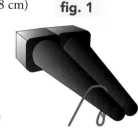

fig. 1

Large rubberized pliers

Round-nose pliers

Chain-nose pliers

2. Cut the chain into two segments of 4 inches (10.2 cm) each. Then cut each of these two 4-inch (10.2 cm) segments into six smaller segments with the following lengths: 1¼ inches (3.2 cm), 1 inch (2.5 cm), 1 inch (2.5 cm), ½ inch (1.3 cm), ⅛ inch (3 mm), and ⅛ inch (3 mm). Keep these lengths of chain separate, being careful not to mix them. Each group of six segments will be used to make one earring.

3. Using the 26-gauge wire, make a loop about ½ inch (1.3 cm) from the end. Slide this loop onto the earring. Grab the loop with the chain-nose pliers and wrap the wire around to secure.

4. Place one 10-mm copper-colored pearl onto this wire and bend the wire 45°. Using the round-nose pliers, loop it around. Place onto this loop one group of the six chain segments cut in step 2. Hold the loop with the chain-nose pliers and twist the wires around to secure. Cut off the shorter wire end. To add extra looping detail, continue looping the wire around and around until you have your desired look. Cut off the remaining wire. ***Note:*** If the end of the wire sticks out a little after you've cut off the excess, use the chain-nose pliers to push the wire end closer to the wrapped wire.

5. Now that you have all of the major parts in place, add the details. For this design, attach briolettes and beads using wire

loop links and ball-end head pins; feel free to add more, fewer, and even a different set of stones. The briolettes are attached to the bottom links of three different pieces of chain. To attach them, first run the 26-gauge wire through the briolette with ¾ inch (1.9 cm) extending out the other end. Bend both wire ends up until they cross. Twist them around to secure the briolette. Cut off the shorter wire end.

6. Using the round-nose pliers, loop the wire around. Slide this loop onto the bottom link in the selected chain. Hold the loop with the chain-nose pliers and wrap the wire around. To add extra looping detail, continue wrapping the wire around until you have your desired look (figure 2). Cut off the excess wire.

fig. 2

7. For the other three pieces of chain, attach head pins with a mixture of beads. You could use the following combinations: one peridot bead, one pearl, and one peridot bead; one peridot bead, one pearl, and one gold-filled bead; and one peridot bead and one gold-filled bead. Mix and match the beads to create combinations of stones and colors that you like; there is no right or wrong way.

8. After you've selected what you want to use on the head pin, bend it 45°. Loop it around the round-nose pliers and slide it through the bottom link in the selected chain. Hold this loop with the chain-nose pliers and wrap the wire around. Again, feel free to use the extra looping detail here by continuing to loop the wire around a few more times. Cut off the excess wire.

9. For one final detail, attach a few more 4-mm peridot beads to the middle links of some of the pieces of chain. Again, slide the wire through the bead so you have ¾ inch (1.9 cm) extending out the other end. Bend up both wires and twist them around to secure the bead. Cut off the shorter wire end.

10. Using the round-nose pliers, loop the wire around and place this loop on the middle of one of the pieces of chain. Hold this loop with the chain-nose pliers and wrap the wire around. Cut off the excess wire.

11. Repeat the steps to make the second earring.

olé!

You'll be in the mood for a fiesta when you slip on these festive earrings, enhanced with silver wire loops styled on a jig.

Designer: Valérie MacCarthy

Finished size: 3 inches (7.6 cm)

Materials

8 rose quartz briolettes (long), 6 mm

12 cherry quartz briolettes (round), 6 mm

8 clear quartz briolettes (round), 6 mm

2 sterling silver ball-post earrings with open rings

12-inch (30.5 cm) length of 5-mm sterling silver krinkle chain

26-inch (66 cm) length of 22-gauge sterling silver wire

28-inch (71.1 cm) length of 26-gauge sterling silver wire

Tools

Jig with a curved grid

Chain-nose pliers

Round-nose pliers

Wire cutters

Large rubberized round-nose pliers or flat nylon-jaw pliers

Ruler

Designer's Tip

Use a jig with a curved grid to make these earrings. If you don't have one, you can adapt the pattern to a regular jig with straight holes, or you could even create the wire shape using round-nose pliers.

Instructions

1. Place five pegs on the jig (figure 1). Using the 22-gauge wire, beginning about ½ inch (1.3 cm) from the end, wrap the wire around the first peg, over and around the second peg, under and around the third peg, over and around the fourth peg, and under and around the fifth peg (figure 2). Make four of these five-hole wire shapes.

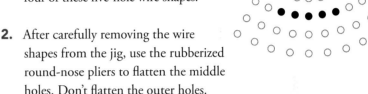

fig. 1

2. After carefully removing the wire shapes from the jig, use the rubberized round-nose pliers to flatten the middle holes. Don't flatten the outer holes.

3. Make two additional shapes, this time using only three pegs instead of five. For these two shapes, wrap the wire over and around, under and around, and over and around (figure 3).

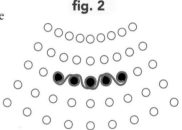

fig. 2

4. Cut the 12 inches (30.5 cm) of chain into twelve 1-inch (2.5 cm) segments. Count the links in the segments to make sure that all of them are exactly the same length.

5. Now the tricky part! Begin attaching these chain segments from the bottom of the earring, working toward the top, first looping the end links of the chain segments into the outer loops of one five-hole wire shape.

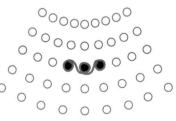

fig. 3

6. After the first two chains are attached to the bottom five-hole wire shape, attach these same chains onto the second five-hole wire shape. Ultimately, these chain ends should lie between the outer two loops on both sides of this second five-hole wire shape (figure 4). It's necessary to keep the chain as straight as possible as you attach it to the next wire shape. It may take a little bit of practice, as well as patience and repetition, to master the technique. Using the chain-nose pliers, close the two outer loops on the lower element.

7. Follow this immediately by attaching two more chains to the outer loops of the second wire shape (figure 5). Then, pushing with the chain-nose pliers, close the two outer wire loops on the second wire shape.

8. Set this piece aside and begin working on the earring from above. Attach two chain segments to one of the three-hole wire shapes. Then pick up the piece from step 7, which has two loose chains at the top, and slide those links onto these same two wire loops (figure 6). Use the chain-nose pliers to close the two outer wire loops on the top-most wire shape.

9. Finally, attach these two chain segments to the ring of the ball-post earring, using the chain-nose pliers

to slightly bend the loop on the ring to one side. Place the two chain segments onto the loop and push the ring back into place. The framework of the earring is now complete.

10. To attach the briolettes, use the 26-gauge wire. Slide the wire through a 6-mm briolette, letting ¾ inch (1.9 cm) of the wire extend out the other side. Bend both wire ends up until they cross tightly. Twist the two wires together. Cut off the shorter wire end.

11. Bend the wire forward 45° and use the round-nose pliers to wrap it around into a loop. Slide the wire through one of the outer loops in the earring framework. Hold this wire loop with the chain-nose pliers and wrap the wire around the twist you made in step 10. Cut off the excess wire.

12. Continue to repeat steps 10 and 11, placing a total of 14 briolettes on the earring, with the four long briolettes in the center of the design. ***Note:*** When attaching the briolettes, all the loops in the briolettes should be side-facing to attach to the holes in the wire shapes, except for the top briolette, which attaches to the ring of the ball-post earring. This one needs a forward-facing loop (figure 7).

13. Repeat steps 5 through 12 to make the second earring.

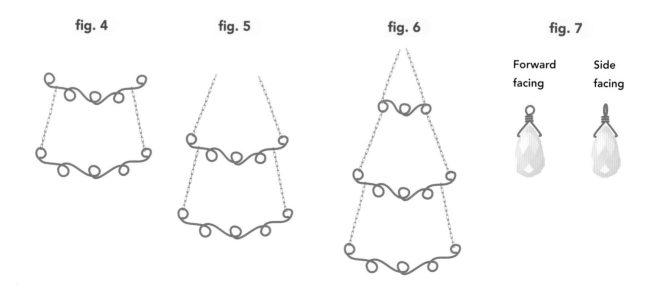

fig. 4 **fig. 5** **fig. 6** **fig. 7**

Forward facing   Side facing

key to wire gauges

The projects in this book were made using wire manufactured in the United States, whose standards for wire diameters differ from those in the British system. AWG is the acronym for American, or Brown & Sharpe, wire gauge sizes and their equivalent rounded metric measurements. SWG is the acronym for the British Standard, or Imperial, system in the UK. Refer to the chart below if you use SWG wire. Only part of the full range of wire gauges that are available from jewelry suppliers is included here.

AWG IN.	AWG MM	GAUGE	SWG IN.	SWG MM
0.204	5.18	4	0.232	5.89
0.182	4.62	5	0.212	5.38
0.162	4.12	6	0.192	4.88
0.144	3.66	7	0.176	4.47
0.129	3.28	8	0.160	4.06
0.114	2.90	9	0.144	3.66
0.102	2.59	10	0.128	3.25
0.091	2.31	11	0.116	2.95
0.081	2.06	12	0.104	2.64
0.072	1.83	13	0.092	2.34
0.064	1.63	14	0.080	2.03
0.057	1.45	15	0.072	1.83
0.051	1.30	16	0.064	1.63
0.045	1.14	17	0.056	1.42
0.040	1.02	18	0.048	1.22
0.036	0.914	19	0.040	1.02
0.032	0.813	20	0.036	0.914
0.029	0.737	21	0.032	0.813
0.025	0.635	22	0.028	0.711
0.023	0.584	23	0.024	0.610
0.020	0.508	24	0.022	0.559
0.018	0.457	25	0.020	0.508
0.016	0.406	26	0.018	0.457

about the designers

Kimberley Adams is a lampwork bead artist who also designs jewelry for the distinctive beads she creates. She's the author of the Lark Jewelry & Beading title *The Complete Book of Glass Beadmaking* and teaches at her own studio in Hendersonville, North Carolina, and other locations. Kimberley is a featured artist in many galleries. Her website is www.kimberleyadams.homestead.com.

Sharon Bateman is a multi-media artist experienced in illustration, airbrush, painting, and carving as well as jewelry and beading. She is best known for her many articles and books, including *Contemporary Loom Beading* and *Findings & Finishings: A Beadwork How-To Book.* Sharon can be reached for questions or comments at www.sharonbateman.com.

Lisa M. Call is a jewelry designer who has been creating and crafting in an array of media all her life. She left the corporate world to raise her daughters and find time for other interests. Wirework, metal, and beads are her main passions, and she has spent the last several years focusing on metalsmithing, wireworking, and beading. Lisa is also a certified Precious Metal Clay artisan. Contact her at www.jewelrybylisamarie.com.

Bonnie Clewans is an international author, designer, and educator. She has appeared on the DIY Channel's *Jewelry Making* show and on local television in Buffalo, New York, and Phoenix, Arizona. Bonnie has taught at the Bead&Button Show, International Quilt Festival, Bead Expo, Bead Fest, and the Creative Needlework and Sewing Festival. She serves as a consultant to Touchstone Crystal and is a Create Your Style Ambassador with Swarovski Elements. To see more of her work, go to www.bonnieclewans.com.

Candie Cooper is a jewelry designer who loves unique materials and color combinations inspired by her years in China. She's the author of several Lark Crafts titles: *Metalworking 101 for Beaders, Felted Jewelry,* and *Designer Needle Felting.* She has also contributed to other Lark books, including *Fabulous Jewelry from Found Objects, Beading with Crystals, Beading with World Beads,* and *Beading with Charms.* She creates designs for craft-industry companies, publications, and on-air talent. Candie teaches workshops internationally and has appeared on PBS. For further information, visit www.candiecooper.com.

Patty Cox developed nearly half of the projects included in *Dazzling Bead & Wire Crafts.* Her 25 designs for that book included jewelry, napkin rings, a picture frame, cocktail skewers, a clock, and a bookmark.

Cynthia Deis has been making tiny things since childhood, when she took apart garage-sale jewelry to create new trinkets for her dolls. She worked as a teacher and as a window dresser before selling her jewelry professionally under the trade name Bedizen Ornaments. She currently lives in Raleigh, North Carolina, where she writes a mixed-media craft blog, teaches, and works in her bead store. Cynthia's website is www.ornamentea.com.

Rachel M. Dow specializes in fabricated sterling silver, metal clay, and found-object jewelry. She also makes handspun, hand-dyed yarn. Her work is shown in selected galleries and at www.rmddesigns.com.

Kate Drew-Wilkinson was born and raised in England and began her professional life as an actress. However, she was always fascinated by the history and magic of beads, and during her travels in many countries, she studied their use in jewelry. By 1990, Kate had discovered the joy of lampworking. She has written two books on bead jewelry, 48 articles for *Lapidary Journal,* and she also makes instructional films. Kate teaches bead jewelry design and lampworked bead making in Europe. Visit http://katedrew-wilkinson.com.

Kathy Frey is an artist in all aspects of her life. For most of her adult life she lived in the urban landscapes of Pittsburgh, Boston, and Chicago. In 2009, she moved to a small artists' community in rural California so she could commune with nature on a regular basis. She enjoys cooking, gardening, and home decorating. When she's not working in her adorable fairy garden/cottage/home studio, she enjoys dancing, yoga, hiking, and snowboarding. All these pursuits are expressed creatively in her sculptural wire jewelry designs, which are abstract expressions of the pleasures she finds in simplicity. Much love goes into creating each piece. Learn more about Kathy via her website, www.kathyfrey.com, where there's also a link to her "Taming the Tangle" blog.

Ellen Gerritse has travelled extensively and taught fine arts in Europe and Asia. She creates objects from accessible materials with a few tools she has at hand. She won the Collectors' Choice Award during the Mind over Metal show in Houston, Texas. Ellen owns and operates WYTS, a gallery in Middelburg, Netherlands. View her work at www.ellengerritse.kunstinzicht.nl.

Tamara Honaman has been immersed in jewelry making and design for more than 15 years. A freelance designer, writer, and instructor, she's also a certified PMC and Senior Art Clay instructor. Tamara is the founding editor of *Step by Step Beads* (now *Beadwork*) and three other publications. She's appeared on the PBS and DIY channels. You can find instructional videos on her DVD *Secrets to Art Clay Success* and through Fire Mountain Gems and Beads, where she hosts "Ask the Experts." See more at www.thonaman.com.

Nancy Kugel was born and raised in St. Louis, Missouri, and has always had an interest in fine crafts, including needlework, basketry, and metalwork. She discovered her love of beading more than 10 years ago, and finds inspiration everywhere she travels.

Diana Light is an artist who lives in the mountains of western North Carolina, where she creates beauty out of anything she gets her hands on. She's especially attracted to shiny objects and believes a girl can never have too much bling. Diana holds a BFA in painting and printmaking from the University of North Carolina-Greensboro.

Jan Loney is a metal artist whose work ranges in scope from site-specific installations to small-scale sculptural work and jewelry, which she creates in her Pittsburgh, Pennsylvania, studio, Metalier. Her designs and work vary from decorative to functional, and quite often embody both. Jan exhibits her work nationally. Find out more about Jan and her work at www.metalier.com.

Valérie MacCarthy makes jewelry that combines the beauty of nature and the inspiring simplicity of colors and shapes. She got her start in jewelry when her grandmother gave her a box of beads and some string at the age of seven. An opera singer by trade, Valérie authored the Lark Jewelry & Beading book *Beading with Gemstones* and continues to fulfill growing demand for her jewelry. Find out more about Valérie at www.valeriemaccarthy.com.

Melody MacDuffee is a long-time beader and wire-worker. She's the author of four books on beading, wirework, and crochet. She now spends most of her time working on Soul of Somanya, a project she co-founded, which is dedicated to the financial empowerment of disadvantaged youth in the Krobo region of Ghana, West Africa.

Marlynn McNutt is the lead jewelry designer for Fire Mountain Gems and Beads and has created many of the inspirational designs featured on the covers and interior pages of the company's catalogs. An accomplished teacher, she has taught numerous classes for bead shops, small groups, and tours. Marlynn's work has been featured in *Simply Beads* and *Bead Unique* magazines and several books. She has also appeared on eight segments of the show *Beads, Baubles, and Jewels* on the PBS Channel.

Linda Rose Nall has been working with wire since 1989. She now focuses primarily on stained-glass functional items and jewelry.

Eni Oken's jewelry embraces an eclectic mix of techniques and precious materials. Fantasy art, sculpture, architecture, and lace-making techniques all come together in her intricate and ornamental designs. Originally from Brazil, Eni now lives in Los Angeles, where she explores new techniques. She's the founder and developer of www.jewelrylessons.com, a virtual community and marketplace for online lessons.

Thomas Jay Parker specializes in creating one-of-a-kind gemstone and cabochon pendants. His work has evolved into silversmithing, where he employs traditional fabrication techniques. When designing beaded necklaces, he enjoys using natural gemstones to create pieces with an organic feel.

Jean Power is an award-winning jewelry designer, teacher, and writer. She loves all aspects of beading and jewelry making, from beading and bead embroidery to wirework and chain mail. Contact Jean at www.jeanpower.com.

Anjanette Randolph creates modern metal jewelry to complement the unique styles and spirits of her clients. Inspired by nature, her designs combine simple, organic shapes and bright, bold colors.

Marinda Stewart is a designer, writer, and teacher who resides in Round Rock, Texas. She has many magazine and book contributions, television appearances, and national ads. Her work has appeared in museum and gallery exhibitions and is in the collections of several corporations and celebrities. Her book *Punchneedle: The Complete Guide* was recently published. Marinda currently works with corporate clients, designing and consulting on end uses for their products. Her website is www.marindastewart.com.

Terry Taylor was an author and editor for Lark Crafts for 15 years. His authored works include *The Altered Object*, *Chain Mail Jewelry*, *Artful Paper Dolls*, and *Altered Art*. In Terry's new life, he's studying jewelry in the Professional Crafts Program at Haywood Community College.

additional photo credits

acknowledgments

Deepest appreciation goes to Abby Haffelt, who did all the tugging and wrestling required to get the manuscript for this book pulled together. Art intern Maegan Zigarevich had the gargantuan task of hunting down all the raw materials that were needed. Carol Barnao took all of those building blocks and fashioned them into a beautiful volume.

And it goes without saying, if the talented men and women who shared their designs in these pages hadn't done so, this book wouldn't exist, and the world's lobes would be just a little worse off for it.

index

project index

This list will help you find projects made using specific types of beads or techniques; you'll find it helpful if you already know the primary kinds of materials or processes you want to use to make your earrings.